LOUNA LAHTI

ALVAR AALTO

1898–1976

Paradise for the man in the street

TASCHEN

Page 2 ▶ Portrait of Alvar Aalto
Page 4 ▶ Experimental Summer House at
Muuratsalo, site plan

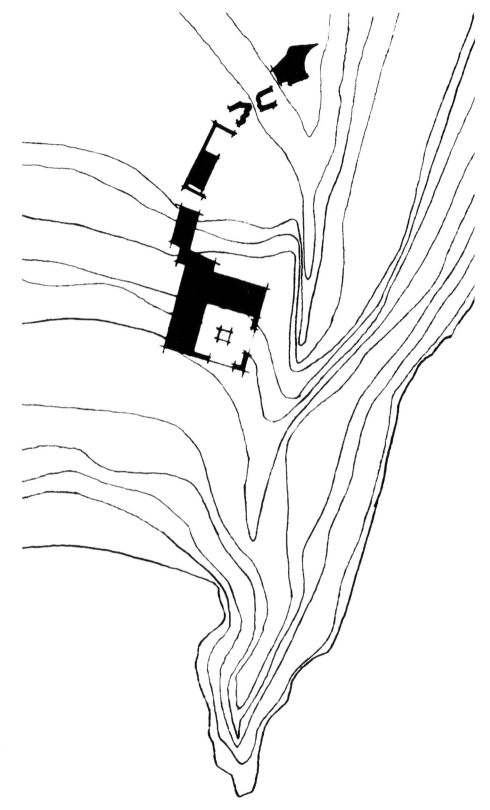

© 2015 TASCHEN GmbH
Hohenzollernring 53, D-50672 Köln
www.taschen.com

© 2015 The Alvar Aalto Museum, photographers

Original edition ▶ ©2004 TASCHEN GmbH
Editor ▶ Peter Gössel, Bremen
Layout ▶ Gössel und Partner, Bremen
Project Manager ▶ Swantje Schmidt, Bremen
Translation ▶ Latido, Bremen

Printed in Slovakia
ISBN 978–3–8365–6010–8

Contents

6   Introduction

16   Workers' Club
18   Municipal Library
22   Tuberculosis Sanatorium
28   The Founding of Artek
30   Residential Building and Studio
34   The Savoy Vase
36   Cellulose Factory and Housing Area
40   Villa Mairea
48   Finnish Pavilion
50   Student Dormitory "Baker House"
54   Säynätsalo Town Hall
58   Institute of Technology
62   Pedagogical University
66   Town Centre
70   Experimental Summer House
74   "House of Culture"
78   Hansaviertel Block of Flats
80   Church of the Three Crosses
84   Maison Carré
88   Neue Vahr Block of Flats
90   Finlandia Hall

92   Life and Work
95   Map
96   Bibliography and credits

Introduction

Left page:

Alvar Aalto with his daughter on the terrace of their house, around 1940

Alvar Aalto was born on the 3rd of February 1898 in the village of Kuortane in the south of East Bothnia. His father was a land surveyor and the small Alvar liked to crawl around under his white worktable. When he was four years old, he discovered the surface of the desk and began to sketch his ideas on it. He inherited his father's social attitude, his cosmopolitan air and the habit of dressing himself flawlessly. He got from his mother his liveliness, his creative talent and his anarchistic temperament. From his maternal grandfather, a forest warden, Alvar learned: "The forest can do without man, but man cannot do without the forest." Alvar was the family's first child, and later came two brothers and a sister. The whole family shared a love for nature, for the forests and the fields.

When Alvar was five years old the family moved to Jyväskylä, in the middle of a lake landscape in central Finland. It was in this town, named the "Athens of Finland", that the first Finnish-language grammar school was founded. This fact decidedly influenced the family's choice of where to live. Although Swedish was also spoken in the family, the parents were more Finnish-minded and liberal.

Alvar was very creative at a very young age: he drew portraits of his family members, wrote short texts, showed an interest for theatre and cinema, and was in an amateur theatre group and in various sports clubs. He received painting instruction and piano lessons. Reading aloud from books was a favourite pastime at home; his favourite author of world literature was Anatole France. While in the first few years at school, he drew a plan for a four-storey snow castle. It was realised on the Harju, a mound of glacial gravel, near his parents' house. From time to time the boy thought of becoming a painter, when not of becoming an architect. When he was eight years old, Alvar suffered a bitter loss with the sudden death of his mother. Her sister, Flora, took her place and became their beloved "Mammu".

At grammar school Alvar received a classical education, and the humanistic spirit left traces behind. In his speech at the centenary celebrations of his school in 1958, Aalto, now professor and member of the Finnish Academy, emphasised the mystical factor called culture that cannot be acquired by the blunt memorising of facts. He praised his school for "the gift of doubt it passed down to me as an inheritance". In 1916, Alvar passed his final examination. He received the best grade in both German and Finnish class in spite of his dyslexia. In the summer after his final examination he gained work experience under the architect Salervo, who gave him the smug advice: "You wouldn't make a good architect, but go ahead and try becoming a newspaper editor!" The piqued young man nevertheless decided to deliver proof of his ability.

After his matriculation he went to study at the Helsinki Institute (now University) of Technology. His father sent him on his way with a word of advice: "Always remain a gentleman!" He was the charmer of the architects, a master of light-hearted celebration and was very popular among his fellow female students. Once, he was brought to jail in tails, where he began writing a book with the title *The Engineer's Sons and Their Sister*. The treatise was confiscated. The incident happened due to civil war; he spent about a fortnight in jail because of a suspicion that he belonged to the right-wing Jaeger movement.

In 1918 his studies were interrupted by the civil war. The war triggered such strong feelings in Aalto that he later had serious difficulties coming to terms with the Second World War. Aalto's father bought a house in Alajärvi and Aalto was commissioned to draw up the plans for the renovation. This renovation of Mammula was his first realised building plan. To his father he wrote: "In theory I'm a damn liberal and a man of the opposition, but in practice I'm an architect and in general a great guy!"

Two of Aalto's teachers at the Helsinki Institute of Technology were the "cornerstones" of his education: Usko Nyström introduced him to the architecture of antiquity and the Middle Ages, and Armas Lindgren introduced him to modern architecture and building and construction theory. It was a lively time: cultural life was blooming, people were travelling abroad and sketching nude models. In 1921, Aalto finished his studies. During a trip to Riga he took part in an art exhibition as an amateur painter, and in Helsinki he worked as a freelance architect and art critic. In 1922, Aalto went to Hamina into a school for reserve officers as part of his military service, where he was discharged from service in the following year as a sergeant. According to his sister, he was the most frequently punished recruit in the school.

His work as an architect in Helsinki was having problems getting off the ground, so he went back to Jyväskylä and founded an architectural office in the basement of the finest hotel in the town. He painted on the timber fence of the hotel, in huge letters: ALVAR AALTO OFFICE FOR ARCHITECTURE AND MONUMENTAL ART. From 1923 to 1927 Aalto worked here with his assistants and published texts under the pseudonym "Remus" for the daily newspaper Sisä-Suomi, texts that have still not lost their relevance.

In 1923 the architect Aino Marsino was hired by the Aalto Office and quickly gained a position of trust. She was given responsibility for the key to the cash box. Alluding to this, Aalto asked for her hand in marriage, and they were married in 1924. After returning from their honeymoon in 1925 the young couple settled down into a single-family home, designed by the architect Wivi Lönn, in a garden city south of Jyväskylä. This cosy and attractive house certainly had an influence on Aalto's future single-family home designs. From the kitchen window Aalto could see the hill on which he was later to build the University of Jyväskylä campus. Later, during the early 1970s, the Alvar-Aalto-Museum was built nearby, a stone's throw away from the house. In 1926 the Aaltos built a summer house in Alajärvi from Aino's sketches, the Villa Flora, in which the couple led a very modern life. It was even rumoured to be a nudist camp, as they did some unusual sunbathing for that time period.

The young couple flew to Italy for their honeymoon, which was out of the ordinary for that time, and spent one and a half months in the warm Mediterranean climate. Italy made an impression on both of them, and this fascination stayed with them for the rest of their lives. They brought Italian chairs back with them for a table that Aalto had designed; these can be seen today in the Aalto House on Riihitie in Helsinki.

In August of 1925, their daughter Hanni was born. It was a productive and happy time. The Workers' Club and Theatre in Jyväskylä and the church in Muurame were realised. In just under four years, Aalto drew 36 sketches, of which 14 were carried out. He wrote in 1921: "In the days before printing, people needed—as symbols of their spiritual ideas in order to satisfy their longing for beauty—large and, above all, pretty buildings. Temples, cathedrals, forums, theatres and palaces related history with more clarity and sensitivity than old rolls of parchment ever could. There was but one art in the

Muurrame Church, 1926–1929
View from the west and from the north

world, the art of building. Painting and sculpture, in all their various forms, blended into it harmoniously; even music was like part of the arched vaults of a Gothic cathedral."

In 1926 Aalto took a trip to Denmark and Sweden, where he met Gunnar Asplund and Sven Markelius. His relationship to Stockholm, which lay on the other side of the Gulf of Bothnia on Swedish shore, intensified as time passed. Gunnar Asplund became a lifelong friend. Aalto even had his suits cut in Stockholm, and the bills from this were by no means trivial. The habit persisted: between fittings years could go by, but with the help of morning gymnastics, his figure remained the same. Denmark fascinated Aalto as well, and he opined that the Finns could learn much from the cosy, petty bourgeois Danish flats.

In 1927 the family moved to Turku in south-western Finland, where a son was born in 1928 and baptised with the name Hamilkar, after his maternal grandfather. The planning for the editorial building of the newspaper Turun Sanomat and for the Agriculture Cooperative Building was approaching. The Paimio Tuberculosis Sanatorium was to prove to be the most important building, with which Aalto was to rise as a functionalist among the most renowned architects of the century.

In 1928 the Aaltos took another road trip, this time with their new Fiat through Sweden and Denmark to Holland, and from there further on to France. Their circle of friends grew to include significant colleagues: Le Corbusier, Johannes Duiker, Sigfried Giedion, Fernand Léger and, from the Bauhaus, László Moholy-Nagy. The meetings of the CIAM in Germany, Greece and Switzerland brought Walter Gropius and Karl Moser as new contacts as well. "The new style is international. And climate doesn't make any significant differences ... he who is great has the confidence to be cosmopolitan, and his own personality will shine through in his work in spite of this."

Aalto's friendship with the architect Erik Bryggman and his wife Agda was very important for him. In 1929 Aalto designed the Turku 700th Anniversary Exhibition with Bryggman and planned the booth of the furniture manufacturer Korhonen. The wood-bending experiments with the furniture manufacturer Otto Korhonen, which had already

begun earlier, were resumed. Friends tested the durability of his stool, which had three L-shaped legs, by tossing it back and forth, whereby Aalto remarked: "Hey, Otto: this stool will be sold to thousands of people!" He was wrong: in the last seventy years, the stool has been bought by millions. In Switzerland, the firm Wohnbedarf began selling Aalto furniture. His success at glass competitions at home opened up new possibilities. During his countless travels, Aalto's theoretical ruminations developed: "A wilful search for new forms can turn up nothing complete ... Only at that point when the form and the content to a certain extent come into being at the same time or are born as a committed togetherness can one speak of a positive step... ."

Street façade of the "Turun Sanomat" newspaper offices

One reason why the couple moved to Helsinki in 1933 was the commission to build the library for the town of Viipuri in south-eastern Finland. Aalto began next with his architectural office in a normal house. Soon the family bought a plot of land in Munkkiniemi, Helsinki. During the building phase of the library in Viipuri, Aalto's office was on an island in the Gulf of Finland; the family spent unforgettable summers on the Carelian Isthmus. Today, Viipuri is part of Russia. Between 1935 and 1936 their house, which the Aaltos designed themselves, was built in Helsinki, and a few of its rooms became the office. Aino overtook the planning and the realisation of the garden. At the beginning the inhabitants could still enjoy the view of the sea, unobscured by buildings.

On October 15th 1935, the Aaltos, Maire Gullichsen and Nils Gustav Hahl founded the furniture company Artek. The main function of the company, whose product line was essentially organised by Aalto's wife Aino, was to market the Aaltos' products. Their furniture design had gained significance after the construction of the sanatorium in Paimio and the library in Viipuri. Aalto had switched from steel to wood. They designed glass objects both together and independently, with Aino additionally designing cloth patterns and Alvar designing light fixtures.

In the founding year of Artek, the married couple travelled once again to central Europe, with Alvar travelling alone further on to London. In 1937, the Finnish Pavilion

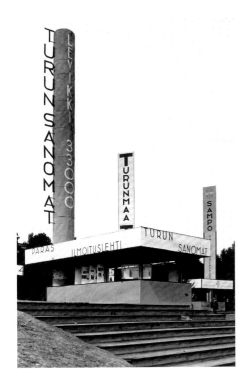

Exhibition building of the newspaper "Turun Sanomat", 1929
Aalto was responsible for the typography here.

at the Paris World's Fair was completed, the architectural competition which Aalto had won. "The exhibition was a great success—all of the glass objects were stolen," remarked Aalto. During a competition for the New York World's Fair in 1939, the Aalto Office won two first prizes, and Aino took third place with her own suggestion. In the suggestion that was carried out, the idea of the curved ceiling from the lyceum of the library in Viipuri was taken up again, now in the form of a wavy exhibition wall, on which large-format pictures were presented on several floors. Aalto later used the motif of forming a wall like the light curtain of the northern lights in smaller format in the museum named after him. In his speech "Rationalism and Man" of 1935, Aalto observed: "The things that surround man are hardly fetishes or allegories that have a mystical eternal value; more than anything else, they are cells and tissues, living beings, building components that make up human life. They cannot be treated differently from other biological units, lest they run the risk of not fitting into the system and becoming dehumanised."

At a 1938 speech at the Nordic Architectural Conference in Oslo, Aalto expressed: "I have said before that nature herself is the best standardisation committee in the world, but in nature, standardisation is almost exclusively applied to the smallest possible unit, the cell. This results in millions of flexible combinations that never become schematic. It also results in unlimited riches and perpetual variation in organically growing forms. We must follow the same path in architectural standardisation, too."

In 1938 the Aaltos took their first trip to America, where the pavilion for the New York World's Fair had just been built. In addition, an exhibition of Aalto's architecture and his furniture was taking place in the Museum of Modern Art. Together with Fernand Léger, Aalto made a speech at Yale University, and in spite of his unclear pronunciation, it was a big success. During their second trip to America in 1939, among those present were Maire and Harry Gullichsen, for whom Aalto had just built the Villa Mairea.

The Helsinki Housing Construction Exhibition of 1939 took place on Aalto's own initiative. After the outbreak of war he was sent to Switzerland to give a lecture about

Gunnar Asplund, Stockholm Exhibition, 1930

the reconstruction. In March of 1940 Aalto and his family travelled to Washington, where he gave lectures about war propaganda. When the family returned from this trip, they immediately became mixed up in the turmoil of the war. Aalto was not drafted into military service. He used the significant connections that he had made in the USA and Switzerland to help his country. In 1943 he was chosen to be chairman of the Finnish Association of Architects (SAFA) and kept this position until 1958. One delegation of the Association travelled to Germany under Aalto's leadership in order to learn about the standardisation work of Ernst Neufert. Aalto is said to have had an influence on the freeing of the architect Nils Koppel, whom the Gestapo had jailed. Later, during Aalto's Swedish construction projects, Koppel became his assistant. One speech that Alvar Aalto gave before the German Supreme Command has become famous, in which he declared to have read Mein Kampf in an American hotel room. In spite of the war Aalto took part in the 1944 exhibition "Vi bor i Friluftstaden" (We live in the outdoor city) in Sweden; in the same year the exhibition "Amerikka rakentaa" (America builds) came at his instigation to Helsinki. In 1947 an exhibition about Alvar and Aino Aalto's 25-year collaboration took place in Helsinki, and afterwards travelled to other European countries.

After the end of the war, Aalto became a professor in the USA at the Massachusetts Institute of Technology (MIT). He was commissioned to plan a student dormitory at MIT. Aalto did not like the American lifestyle: he found it too superficial and thus returned to Finland in 1948. Shortly after returning, Aino died of a serious illness, a great tragedy for Alvar Aalto. Aalto tried to overcome the depression caused by Aino's death with work, wine and travels. In 1950 a retrospective of the entire architectural work of Aino and Alvar Aalto was shown at the Galérie Foch in Paris, but Aalto "forgot" to appear at the formal reception for the opening. One year prior he had gained one of his most important victories at an architecture competition under the pseudonym "Curia". This was the Säynätsalo Town Hall, built 1950–1952. Red brick walls became his passion.

In the middle of this phase, a new love appeared in Aalto's life. The young architect Elissa Mäkiniemi and Alvar Aalto were married on the 4th of October 1952. The con-

struction of the Säynätsalo Town Hall inspired the newlywed couple to acquire a plot of land on a neighbouring island. There they built a summer home, now known as the Experimental Summer House at Muuratsalo. Aalto even planned a motorboat for the trip to the island with the name "Nemo propheta in patria" (No one is a prophet in his own country).

Aalto's own House on Riihitie remained the only realised Aalto building in the capital city region for a long time. Aalto's first public building in Helsinki was the entrance to the air-raid shelter on Erottaja Street (1949–1951), which was named "Kiosk", or, popularly, even "Pissoir". Later, outstanding works by Aalto appeared in the city of red brick, in copper gloss or even covered with marble, like the National Pensions Institute, the Rautatalo Office Building and the Finlandia Hall.

In 1955 Aalto was named a member of the Finnish Academy and became its president in 1963. The topic of his inaugural lecture was "Art and Technology". Aalto held this seat until 1968. The Aalto Architectural Office experienced a hectic time during the 1950s and 1960s, starting in 1955 in the new studio, Tiilmäki, near the House on Riihitie. The Artek 20th Anniversary Exhibition was shown in Helsinki. When the Rautatalo Office Building was completed, business rooms of the company were opened in it. At the opening Aalto scoffed: "I had the inner courtyard dimensioned in such a way that the Helsinki intellectuals, and only they, fit inside." The productivity of the Aalto Office rose tremendously in the last years, both in quantity and quality, which, according to Aalto's words, was the only measure of art. Cultural buildings in various regions of Finland and Europe, and of course homes for friends, as well as churches, plans for universities, housing estates, city centres and zoning plans were among the productions. Even Farah Diba, spouse of the Persian Shah and herself an architect, inspired her husband to commission an art museum from Aalto, of which, however, only a plan on paper has remained.

Shortly before his death, Aalto learned that a church based on his designs was to be built in Riola, Italy. Up until that point the only churches of his design realised outside of Finland were in Germany, where his architecture was also appreciated; lastly, the Alvar Aalto Theatre was completed in Essen, Germany posthumously. In his later years he received countless gold medals, honorary doctorates and similar distinctions from all over the world—so many that he spoke of the "triviality of notoriety". After his death, his plans for the church were not carried out until 1994, when Elissa Aalto, who led the office with Aalto's nephew Heikki Tarkka, died. Today the Alvar Aalto Foundation is located in the Aalto Studio on Tiilimäki; the Aalto House on Riihitie is open to the public as a museum.

Alvar Aalto died in Helsinki on the 11th of May 1976. He was buried in the historic Hietaniemi Cemetery next to Aino Aalto. Elissa Aalto was laid to rest next to him in 1994.

In his youth, Aalto had learned about Nordic classicism, to which he devoted himself in the 1920s. This style paved the way for functionalism, which first becomes visible in the Turun Sanomat Newspaper Offices. But the conventions of functionalism were not enough for Aalto who detested every kind of prescription. "It makes no sense to develop new forms when there is no new content," he stated in 1927. This thought arose from the teachings of the Bauhaus. In 1935 he even attacked the basic idea behind functionalism and warned: "Architecture does not just encompass all of the spheres of human life; it must also be developed further in all of these spheres at the same time. Should this not happen, we will only get one-sided and superficial results."

Organic architecture became manifest in the Villa Mairea. "The form is a mystery that eludes every definition." At the end of the 1940s, the red brick period began. At the end of the 1950s, plastic, whitewashed buildings appeared in his work, whose use in large administrative and cultural centres, proved his genius. "And yet the status of public buildings in society should be just as important as the role of the vital organs in the human body, if we do not wish our societies to become polluted by traffic, psychologically repulsive and physically stressful," Aalto concluded in 1953. He always underlined the responsibility of the architect to be a servant of society; "the man in the street" was always the measure of his planning: "I have the feeling that there are many situations in life in which organisation is too brutal; the duty of the architect is to give life a more sensitive structure."

Aalto emphasised that his furniture and sculptures arose as a part of architecture. "My furniture rarely, if ever, arises as a result of professional design. Almost without exception, I have designed it in conjunction with architectural projects...." Aalto spoke fondly of the "charm that enriches life that is imperative for artistic creating and planning".

Finnish Pavilion at the Biennale in Venice, Italy, 1955/56
Today this small building serves as the Icelandic pavilion, while Finland is accommodated in a newer, joint building for Scandinavia by Sverre Fehn.

Church in Riola di Vergato, 1966–1994
Vezio Nava, a former colleague of Aalto, oversaw the construction.

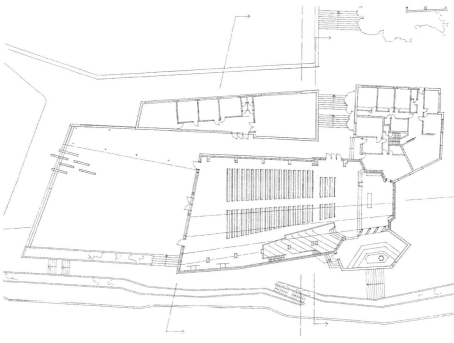

Church in Riola
Plan

1924–1925 · Workers' Club
Jyväskylä, Finland

View from the street

Left page:
Interior view

Floor plan

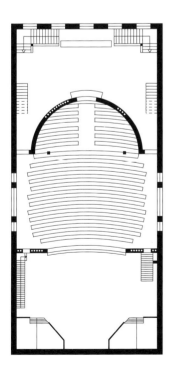

In various phases of his creation, Alvar Aalto repeatedly referred to the inspirational effect of the landscape and architecture of the Mediterranean countries, especially Italy. Venice, with its palaces and canals, the Cappella Pazzi in Florence and the mediaeval Architettura minore, the anonymous small-town architecture, were close to his heart. He wanted to make a Mediterranean hilltop town, a Florence of the North, out of his home city Jyväskylä .

Aalto's first public building was the Workers' Club and Theatre in Jyväskylä. The planning began at the start of 1924, and in the following year the edifice was completed. One can discover traces of the old Southern building culture on the Workers' Club, transferred onto the classicist spirit that dominated in Finland in the 1920s.

Aalto had concerns about constructing a public building on a corner site. It was usual for important buildings to be located in parks or at least to have an obvious main façade. Workers' Club was therefore a challenge.

The plan commissioned by the workers' union foresaw a café and a restaurant on the ground floor, and above it, on the first floor, a theatre hall. The main façade of the building, with its Venetian influences, is dominated by the ceremonial balcony with its multi-paned window. The balcony has no practical function; it is a part of the asymmetrical composition of the façade, as are the other decorative elements. The second side that faces the street is strictly symmetrical. Both façades have windows on the ground floor surrounded by Doric columns. Aalto designed the third, short side as an end to a ceremonial yard of the spacious site. The result is a "Palazzo alle colonne" in the size of a small town in central Finland.

The fundamental idea of the Workers' Club follows the classic type of a 19th century theatre: the entrance and service rooms are located on the ground floor, from which one goes up stairs and comes to the foyer and the theatre itself. The stairway is dominated by classical details and by a symmetrical, semicircular window. The main entrance to the theatre hall is located in the middle of a curved wall that runs throughout the building, the central architectural element of the foyer. This wall and its paintings are almost directly borrowed from Leon Battista Alberti, a Renaissance architect whom Aalto greatly admired. Aalto used traditional forms for lighting and other details.

It may be questionable whether a classically refined language of forms fits in with the democratic spirit of a workers' union. Yet Aalto succeeded in answering this skilfully. He broke through the strict symmetry in multiple places and emphasised man as measure. The Workers' Club and Theatre was Aalto's first cultural centre and multipurpose building, in which the central elements of his later designs are already present in seed.

1927–1935 ‣ Municipal Library
Viipuri, Russia

Rear of the building

Left page:
The glassed-in stairwell

Ground floor plan

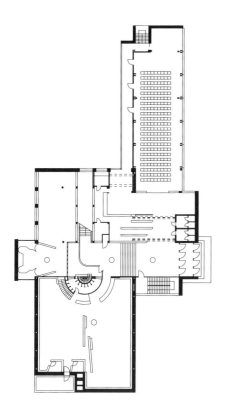

At the end of the 1920s, Viipuri was, with almost 90,000 inhabitants, the second largest city in Finland. In 1927 Alvar Aalto won the planning competition for the library with his design entitled "V.V.V." Originally, the planned building site was located on a street. Aalto's first suggestion was drawn in neo-classical style; one can see similarities to Gunnar Asplund's City Library in Stockholm. In the autumn of the previous year Aalto had travelled to Sweden and Denmark and had met Gunnar Asplund, among others. In the next year Aalto worked on his plan and removed all of the neo-classical elements. In 1929 a third version arose, according to which the library was to be conjoined with the cultural centre across the street. However, due to the economic crisis, the construction was delayed.

In the autumn of 1933 the city council decided on Torkkeli Park as the new location for the library. In the same year Aalto sketched a new version. Altogether there are four completely different designs from Aalto's hand, where the first three rather represent unrealised plans as beginning stages of the final, completed library building. In 1934 the construction was begun, and in October of 1935 the building was ready to be officially opened.

The library is composed of two overlapping blocks. The actual library is located in one, the auditorium in the other. The façades are plastered white. The building has three entrances: the main entrance to the north, the door to the street on the eastern side, through which one reaches the reading room, and the southern door leading from the playground to the children's section. The main entrance is located where the two parts of the building meet. The stair, visible behind a glass wall, leads to the upper level. Aalto is said to have commented that his wife designed the most beautiful staircase in the world: the staircase of the Viipuri Municipal Library.

Seen from the outside, the building has a rather closed effect. The interior dimensions are characterised by alternating level heights. The auditorium can be reached via the large hall. The purpose of the now-famous wavy, wood-panelled ceiling is to improve the acoustics of the auditorium. Unlike concert halls, it works in both directions, so that reciprocal communication is facilitated. The actual library is formed by a large hall that is divided into issuing and reading rooms by means of varying levels and curtains. The free-standing executive office is located on a platform in the centre of the hall. Aalto was especially interested in questions of lighting. The cylindrical skylights are the central theme of the roomy and bright library hall. Yet because they rise up out of the roofage, the roof garden of the original plan had to be scratched. There are altogether 57 round skylights in the hall, each measuring 1.8 metres in diameter. Streams of sunlight are spread wide by the depth of the cylinders—the books are thus protected from direct sunlight and the reader is not disturbed by shadow phenomena that would arise due to direct light.

In addition to the floating ceiling of the auditorium, Aalto also designed the details of the furnishings: bookshelves, counters, wall panels, detached separating walls and, as the highlight of his lighting planning, the adjustable, light-diffusing lamps of a

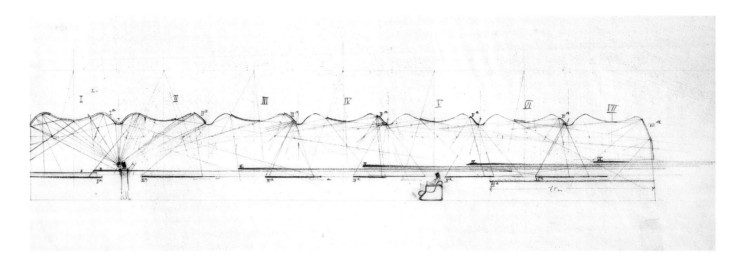

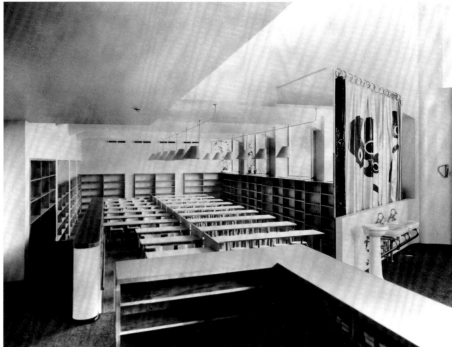

Top left:
Entrance hall
Aalto later mounted the door handles at the Institute of Pedagogics in Jyväskylä in a similar fashion.

Top right:
Childrens' library

special design. Altogether, six different types of wood were used in the furnishing. The entire building services were built into the 75-centimetre-thick exterior brick walls, for example the ducts of the mechanised mechanical ventilation system, which was innovative for its time, and the heating and water pipes. In the library section, flat-panel radiators are built into the pre-stressed concrete ceiling, and so there is a dense network of heating pipes behind the ceiling surface.

Viipuri, like all of Carelia, fell to the Soviets as a result of the Second World War, and today the city belongs to Russia. The Aalto Library suffered much during Soviet times, but was still used as it was originally intended. After the fall of the Iron Curtain an international foundation collected money for the restoration of the library, yet the renovation has been delayed for financial reasons.

This chair, developed for Viipuri, linked the later purely geometric forms and classical furniture.
It is still in production today, slightly modified.

1928–1933 ▸ Tuberculosis Sanatorium
Paimio, Finland

Rear of the building with power station

Left page:
View from the outside

Just as in the rest of the world, Finland was engaged in a battle against tuberculosis before the Second World War. The planning competition for the Tuberculosis Sanatorium in Paimio, south-western Finland, approximately thirty kilometres from the city of Turku, was announced in 1928, and the result was made public in the following year. Aalto won with his design: he had marked his plans with a symbol that depicted a window in the shape of an L. Aalto borrowed the idea of L-shaped windows for the patients' rooms from André Lurçat. During the construction, however, they were substituted with traditional rectangular windows for practical reasons. The brick pitched roof of the main building and the brick pent roofs of the surrounding personnel houses were likewise replaced with flat roofs.

In the plan based on his contest entry, Aalto had the various functions divided among four building parts, grouped around the entrance: the main part, consisting of the patients' wing and the resting ward wing, the social and administrative wing, the service wing behind it to the east and the central heating plant. The elevators and stairwells that lead to the upper levels are located in the entry area connecting these building sections.

The six-storey patients' wing that opens southward to the light and the resting ward wing diagonally connected to it dominate the building complex. A short building is located to the north, in which a canteen, a kitchen and common rooms are housed. A perspective optical illusion in the Cour d'honneur tradition was chosen as a solution for the yard between these building parts.

After the city of Turku had decided to take part in the project, the rising demand for space necessitated that the sanatorium, built 1929–1932, receive three more storeys

Lounge
Not only did Aalto remodel all of the furniture for Paimio, but even individual models for each room.

Chair for Paimio, model no. 41

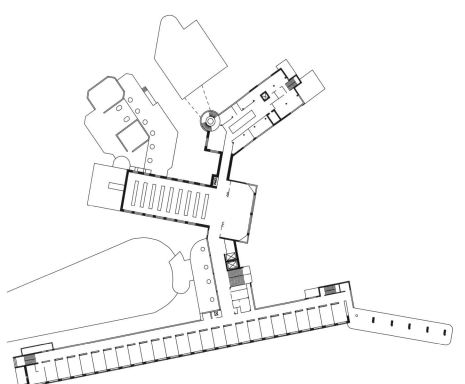

Plan

The outdoor balcony with view of the
meandering garden paths

than originally conceived. The construction consists of a concrete-pillared building
structure and exterior walls built of brick. The resting ward wing is an exception, which
was at the time of its completion the largest concrete structure poured in one piece in
Finland. Aalto used the reinforced concrete construction as an aesthetic means and let
it stand out visibly. In its original form the sanatorium in Paimio was one of the
buildings that Aalto himself completely furnished. He planned all of the details, from
the spittoons to the washbasins. Many of his most important furnishing ideas can be
associated with this project. Aalto stated that the angle of the seat to the backrest of his
famous Paimio chair was designed to ease the patients' breathing.

During the planning of the patients' rooms Aalto paid special attention to ensuring
that everything be as free of disturbance and as pleasant as possible. The rooms had
ceiling heating and were painted in soft colours. A view of the surrounding pine forests
opened out from the beds and the light sources were located outside the field of vision

of the patients lying in bed. The washbasins were constructed so as to prevent running water from causing any sound or splashing.

The colours that Aalto stipulated were intended to enliven the bare white functionalism of the hospital. The colour scale of the patients' rooms was earth-tone based and the public rooms were bright. Outside, the railings and the awnings of the patients' wing were kept orange. The most well-known detail of the colouring is the yellow stairwell. Inside the building, Aalto used graphics for orientation.

The plan as a whole intended for employees' flats to be built next to the sanatorium building: a single-family home for the leading doctor, row houses for other doctors and a residential building for the administrative employees. A fan-shaped sauna building, a greenhouse and a mortuary are located to the side. A duplex house for doctors and a dormitory for personnel were built later.

In the 1950s Aalto designed a new service wing. In the 1960s the complex was transformed into a normal hospital after the number of tuberculosis infections de-

Ceiling light

clined. A defining change that influenced the appearance of the building was the 1963 conversion of the open resting ward wing to closed-off patients' rooms.

As one of the central buildings of architectural modernity, the sanatorium was already attracting attention before the Second World War. It was Aalto's breakthrough to an international reputation. The complex's renovation into a normal hospital brought with it extensive rebuilding and new structures—yet one of the patients' rooms was kept in its original form.

MEUBLES
MAISON AR

COMPOSITION AINO ET ALVAR AA

1935 · The Founding of Artek

As early as the 1920s, Aalto began designing furniture and other objects. One thing typical of his chairs, tables and church objects from this period is the classical language of forms that Aalto had acquired during his studies. The year 1928 was a decisive one, in which he met the cabinetmaker Otto Korhonen, through whom Aalto became familiar with the character of wood and its possibilities in furniture design. The stackable wood chair, which Aalto used in the Defence Corps Building in Jyväskylä among other places, represents the first fruition of this collaboration. Aalto got to know Bauhaus-style tubular-steel framed furniture during his travels through Europe and from specialist literature as well. In 1928 he even ordered Marcel Breuer's Wassily Chair for his apartment in Turku. His own experiments with furniture with tubular steel frames and a moulded plywood seat were restricted to a few models of chairs and sofas around the end of the 1920s and the beginning of the 1930s.

Aalto's furniture design began to develop independently and individually in connection with the furnishing of the Paimio Tuberculosis Sanatorium: the well-known Paimio Chair resulted in 1932. The wish to create a light, bendable and hygienic piece of furniture, close to nature in its material, that would be well-suited for use in the sanatorium formed the basis for this. Later, the Paimio Chair would become world famous. Yet Aalto's actual invention was the L-shaped leg for a chair or table, made of bent laminated wood, which he himself called "the pillar's little sister" and for which he even got an international patent. This type of chair or table-leg was first mass produced for the 1935 Viipuri Library for the chairs with a low backrest. The most well-known piece of furniture with an L-shaped leg is the stackable three-legged stool, which has been manufactured millions of times.

Aalto's furniture began to appear at exhibitions in various parts of the world at the same time. It made its first significant entrance in London in 1933. During this period Aalto established a name for himself as a designer, though not yet as an architect. His reputation and the clear commercial success of his furniture led to the founding of Artek in 1935. The purpose of the company was, and still is, to market and sell Aalto furniture. At first, Aino Aalto was the artistic director of the company and then managing director of the company from 1940 until her death in 1949. In the drawing office at Artek, variations of and new applications for Aalto's classical models from the 1930s were developed. Among Aalto's own new designs was the Y-leg, which arose when the L-shaped leg was sawed through diagonally. It is used as a leg for a glass table, for example. A second, new version appeared in 1954: the so-called X-leg, a fan shaped variation of the earlier models. An extensive selection of chairs, tables, sofas, cupboards and bookshelves is all part of Artek's Aalto collection. Today, original Aalto furniture from the 1930s has a high value on the antique market.

"Tank" armchair with spring function, no. 400 from 1936

Left page:
Conservatory with furniture by Aino and Alvar Aalto at the Paris World's Fair, 1937

1935–1936 ‣ Residential Building and Studio
Riihitie, Helsinki, Finland

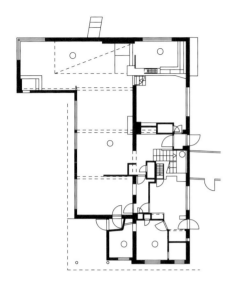

Ground floor plan

Left page:
Work area

View from the garden

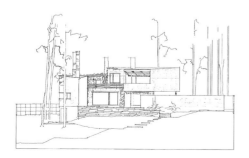

Helsinki, Finland's capital, was Aino Aalto's home town. For Alvar Aalto it was the city in which he had studied and to which he later returned with his family in 1933. In 1934 Alvar Aalto received the commission to draw up the zoning plan for Munkkiniemi, north-west of Helsinki. The project was not realised, but Aalto found a plot of land for his own house in Munkkiniemi. During their first years in Helsinki, the family lived in flats. The planning for their own home and office began in autumn of 1935, and in the following year, the new house was ready to be moved into.

Aalto had already designed several classical single-family homes in the 1920s. Functionalist houses were the predecessors to the House on Riihitie at the beginning of the 1930s, including the House of the Senior Consultant in Paimio and the Villa Tammekann in Estonia. The planning and construction of his own house, however, assumed a key position for Aalto's planning principles and view of living.

Alvar Aalto was an idealist who always emphasised the importance of creating better living conditions and flats for everyone. His thoughts were closely associated with the worldview of affluent Scandinavian society. Yet he was also a realist, who said: "Architecture cannot save the world, but it can set a good example." For Aalto, every building offered the chance to set up an earthly paradise for people.

The summer house Villa Flora in Alajärvi, completed in 1926 and mainly designed by Aino Aalto, as well as their House on Riihitie, were small paradises for the Aalto family. Living in the Munkkiniemi of the 1930s was almost like life in the countryside. One tram did go to Helsinki, but next to the Aalto family house grazed the cows and sheep of a neighbouring estate.

The House on Riihitie was the first of Aalto's buildings that was constructed in the Helsinki region. It became a kind of business card and housed both the private area as well as the architectural office. Aalto underlined this dual purpose in his selection of the materials for the façade: the office wing is made of whitewashed brick, and for the first time, the surface material of the residential wing consisted of narrow, dark wooden slats, which were later to become a central characteristic of his architecture. The flat roof, the roof terrace and the arrangement of the windows still showed a functionalist form, but with this house Aalto freed himself from the dogma of the sterile white box.

Aalto always emphasised the unity of interior and exterior space in his architecture. The living section was built directly on the street so that the interior courtyard opening southward would come forth as largely as possible. The street façade is closed, and this effect is emphasised by the relatively high brick wall that protects the living section. Climbing plants and the natural stone steps that lead to the door take the austerity from the façade.

The interior courtyard borders a rather steep cliff that slopes down toward a sports field. The slat fence alludes to old Finnish architectural traditions and there is a small pool in the yard. The yard is reminiscent in its expression of a Japanese garden, in which the details, restricted to the essential, form a balanced whole.

In spite of the division of the house into a living area and an office area, there is only one entrance, via which the closed character of the façade is further emphasised. The office part is dominated by the studio, which stretches over the height of two storeys. The representation rooms on the ground floor, the large living room and the dining room open via large windows and the door to the interior courtyard. Aalto said: "There has to be a unity between the interior and the exterior of our homes like an elegant, ceremonial form." The yard is a kind of gap, an extension of the interior, an outside living room. A thin plywood sliding door serves as a delimitation from the studio.

The private rooms are on the first floor; the two-storey hall with an open fireplace in the middle serves as the family's actual living space. The bedrooms and the guest room are grouped around this hall, which is brightened by a high-placed window.

There was originally a nice view to the sea from the first storey terrace. In the 1950s, however, multiple dwellings were built, which now block the view. One's attention in the Aalto House on Riihitie is directed toward the light and the air. Especially the rooms on the ground floor merge into each other and open up to the landscape. The cosiness of the entire house is a result of the small, intimate scale and the four simple fireplaces as well as the furnishings, all of which can be seen in its most beautiful form in Aino and Alvar Aalto's furniture design.

Left page:
Terrace on the garden side (top) and corner windows of the office (below)

Above:
Living room

Below:
Garden door handle

Aalto's own house introduces a new phase in his architecture that one could call romantic functionalism. Aalto compared his House on Riihitie to an old Finnish farmhouse, in which simple materials and a simplified, somewhat rough building manner form a harmonious whole. The organic grouping of the rooms, the free form, the use of wood, copper, brick and other natural materials as well as the diversity of sensual details like carefully planned handles and flowerbed borders became his typical elements of style.

1936 ‣ The Savoy Vase

Left page:
Savoy Vase with wood cast form
Vases sold today are formed with steel casting, which gives a smoother, less affected material surface.

Design and architecture are inseparable in Alvar Aalto's creations. It is often difficult—if not impossible—to draw a boundary between them: even fixed, built-in details like door handles became independent objects of design. His world of design and its forms stem from the same source as his architecture. For example, a free, waved line is used on the ceiling of the Viipuri Library, in the swimming pool of the Villa Mairea as well as on this famous glass vase. He used the shape of a fan, inspired by nature, both during extensive plans for a city centre as well as to fit the top and the leg of a piece of furniture together.

During his time of studies, Alvar Aalto was already quite interested in crafts and joined the Finnish Professional Association in 1920. He was only able to begin with glass design in the 1930s, when significant design contests were being organised in Finland. Aino and Alvar Aalto participated in these, both of them under their own names, and their prized objects are still being produced today. Especially Alvar Aalto's so-called Savoy Vase, designed for the Paris World's Fair, has become a design icon of the 20th Century due to its free design. In the years since, several variations have arisen in various colours and sizes.

**Moulded glass from the design "Bölgeblick"
by Aino Aalto, 1932, made by Karhula-Iittala**

1936–1954 ▸ Cellulose Factory and Housing Area
Sunila ▸ Kotka, Finland

Entrance hall of the office building

Left page:
View of the factory from the west
The silo with exposed joints contrasts with the long, red brick buildings on the one hand and the natural cliff on the other.

The Sunila Factory is located on the Gulf of Finland at the mouth of the Kymi River. Today, Sunila is part of the port city Kotka, which lies west of the Kymi Delta. The river used to be an important transport route, via which wood was rafted from the interior of the country to the coast. The location of the factory in the port city was thus logistically very convenient.

Already at the end of the 1920s five large industrial businesses founded the Sunila Corporation, but the building project did not get under way until the second half of the 1930s. During this time Finland's woodworking industry developed rapidly. In those times, firms often built their own living settlements around the factories and commissioned architects not just to design the factory buildings, but also to develop the land-use plans and the residential buildings as well.

In 1936 Aalto was asked to plan the new building of the Cellulose Factory, the zoning plan of the town and the living settlement itself. In 1930 Aalto had designed the Toppila Cellulose Factory in Oulu, the largest city in Northern Finland, and thus he had already gained experience in this field. Aalto had a good personal relationship to the founders of the Sunila Corporation, especially to the director of the A. Ahlström Corporation, Harry Gullichsen, as well as his wife Maire. Aalto worked together with engineers and the factory leadership during the planning. The engineers made important contributions during the planning of the factory and were just as involved in the overall planning as Harry Gullichsen.

The factory was built on an island, the living settlement on a peninsula next to it. Thus production and living as well as work and free time were cleverly separated from each other, according to the principles of functionalist city planning. Aalto began the planning of the factory building in the autumn of 1936 with the technical director, who was responsible for production. Although the planning of the factory had to conform to technical conditions and Aalto's contribution was mainly in the design of the exterior, he tried to bring the industrial architecture in harmony with its surroundings. After the zoning plan was completed in 1936, construction was begun without delay and the factory was completed in two years. Instead of blasting away the island's cliff, the factory was built on it. Aalto wanted the workers in the factory to have a view of the landscape. Standard window elements were used, which were bound to large glass surfaces. On the south-west shore of the island a deep water harbour and a storage facility for the cellulose were built.

The factory was divided into various buildings, in accordance with the manufacturing process, with several warehouses and an office building. Each of the manufacturing buildings has a concrete structure and walls of red brick. The warehouses and the transport system are made of white concrete. Various constructions were tried out for the warehouses. The sodium sulphate repository was constructed with concrete arches in succession. The sulphate repository received a roof made of arches of laminated wood. Aalto also planned the gatehouse and the factory fence. In 1938, the production was launched.

Above:
View of the factory from the east

Right:
Site plan

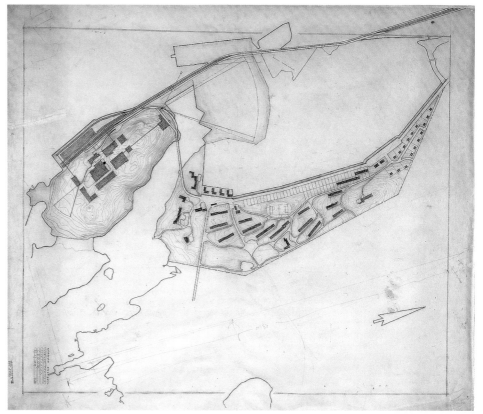

Above:
Row houses
Each unit has three apartments, although each unit has its own entrance.

Below:
Vertical section

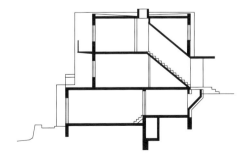

The residential settlement was erected house group after house group between 1936 and 1954. During the first construction phase the residential building and the sauna for the director, the row houses and the sauna for the engineers, the central heating plant, the fire station, the row houses for the foremen, single-family homes, chain-houses, a clubhouse and a sauna for the workers were built. In addition the clubhouse for the executives (named Shanghai) was renovated. In the second phase before the war, more residential buildings and the thermal power station were built. In the 1940s and 1950s the residential and service buildings were erected according to Aalto's plans.

The houses of the residential settlement were placed freely by Aalto in the forest in fan-shaped formation. Aalto experimented with different house types: there were white-plastered two-storey and three-storey flat-roofed row houses and single-family wood homes with pitched roofs. The modernist flat-roofed chain-houses for engineers and workers, built during the first construction phase, are the most well-known. Compared to the traditional planning of factory settlements, the social hierarchy at Sunila does not stand out in particular today. The flats of the directors and engineers have fenced-in gardens; during the planning of the workers' houses, more attention was paid to the communal aspect. The flats of the directors and the engineers have the best location, to the south directly next to the sea—on the other hand, they are also the nearest to the factory. The residential settlement of Sunila, built between the trees, is viewed to be Finland's first satellite city.

1938–1939 ▸ Villa Mairea
Noormarkku, Finland

Entrance with canopy

Left page:
The large living room

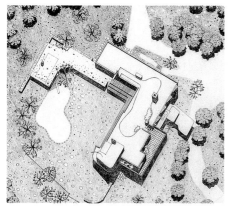

Site plan

In the mid-1930s, Alvar Aalto had the House on Riihitie built for his own use, and it is a quite modest residential and office building. The Villa Mairea in Noormarkku, western Finland, on the other hand, is a luxurious residence, as Aalto was able to let his ideas run free without having to take financial restrictions into consideration.

Maire and Harry Gullichsen, who commissioned Aalto with the Villa Mairea, were friends of the Aalto couple. Maire was the well-to-do heir to the company Ahlström, a lover of art and design and a gallery owner who had far-reaching connections with the European art scene. Her husband Harry Gullichsen was the general director of the A. Ahlström Company. The Gullichsen couple, who were closely associated with the modernism of the 1930s, encouraged Aalto to create something new and extraordinary.

Aalto drew his first proposal at 1:100 scale in the winter of 1938. The plan envisaged an L-shaped building with three storeys on the entrance side and two on the garden side. The garden was encircled by a wall and contained a sauna and a curved swimming pool. An elevated interior hall formed the centre of the house.

Yet already in April of 1938 Aalto signed a change in the plans, taking out the elevated interior hall. The so-called "Proto-Mairea" has varying floor levels, platforms and a score of various guest rooms on the ground floor as well as on the first floor. The art gallery has its own building behind the swimming pool, another remarkable feature.

The excavation of the foundation for the "Proto-Mairea" had already begun when Aalto decided in the spring of 1938 to change the plan once again. The original ground

Above:
Entrance side from southeast

Below:
Narrow side from southwest

floor shape was changed, and the living rooms and the separated art gallery were to be combined into a large multipurpose room. The representation rooms and the function rooms are located on the lower level; on the upper level are the private rooms, the guest rooms and Maire Gullichsen's studio. There are altogether more than four hundred sketches of the house, the last of which are dated January 1939.

The Villa Mairea stands on the knoll of a lightly sloping hill in a pine forest. When one approaches the building, one's first impression is a bright, modernistic façade shimmering between the trees. Coming closer, one gradually becomes aware of the rich details and their metaphorical allusions.

Aalto often emphasised the significance of the transition between the outside and the inside, the "area between" that leads the guest inside from the outside and vice versa. The roofing over the entrance of the Villa Mairea is borne by young tree trunks next to each other, which make the space underneath seem dusky even during the day. Inside the house, one's glance almost immediately encounters another "forest", behind which hides the stairway that leads to the upstairs. Next to this, a broad, bright view of the interior court opens up, which one can conceive of as an allegory of a Finnish beach landscape with a stone wall and a sauna. To the south the view is delimited by a small, artificially placed hill. Aalto had used such forest symbolism for the first time in 1937 for the Pavilion at the Paris World Exhibition.

Garden side with pool

Door handle

Several parallels to Aalto's own house are easy to discover in the Villa Mairea. For example, the public representation rooms and the workrooms are on the ground floor, and the private rooms are on the upper floor; both projects also have in common the use of narrow ribs of dark timber as wall panelling. The turf-covered sauna, the stone wall, the traditional wooden gate and many other solutions allude to traditional Finnish architecture. At the same time one can sense characteristics of old Japanese architecture in the rich details of the house in terms of scale and the use of material. Aalto never visited Japan, but while he was planning the Villa Mairea he wore a kimono, which he had received from a Japanese ambassador as a gift.

The Villa Mairea counts as one of Alvar Aalto's main works, in which he was able to show the full range of his ability. Aalto finally freed himself entirely from formal functionalism and achieved the organic—and ultimately the romantic as well—language of forms in architecture in a way that was to become a signature of his later work. The variety of details and the sensual elegance were, however, unique to Aalto's creations.

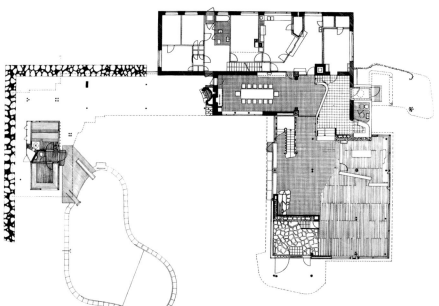

Above:
View from the living area to the sauna

Left:
Floor plan

Right page, top:
Music area with grand piano
The instrument was designed and constructed especially for the Villa Mairea.

Right page, bottom left:
The "forest" around the stair to the top storey

Right page, bottom right:
Top storey floor plan

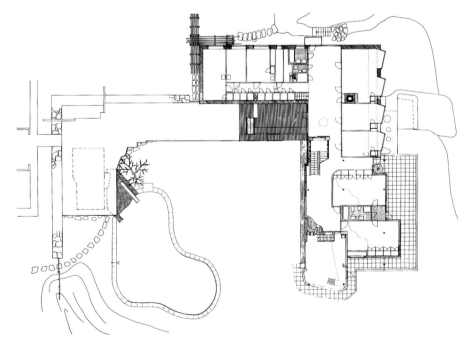

Staircase

Left page:
Studio on the top floor

Garden room

1938–1939 · Finnish Pavilion

Destroyed ▸ World Exhibition ▸ Queens, New York

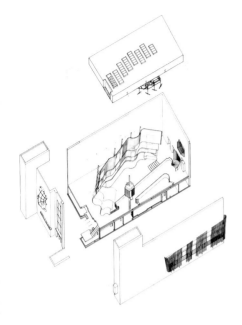

Alvar Aalto and Aino Aalto both took part in this architecture competition, Alvar with two entries and Aino with one. Alvar Aalto won two first prizes and Aino Aalto won the third prize. A ready-made booth stood in the lengthy exhibition hall which the host country had made available to the smaller nations. The aim was thus to design an interior room of small dimensions. Alvar Aalto participated in the competition because here he was able to realise an idea that he had had to drop during the planning of the living space of the Villa Mairea. On one side he placed a wavy surface that tended forward, reminiscent of the northern lights; a curved balcony is located on the wall across from it. An exciting interior courtyard arose as a result. The award-winning proposal contained two alternatives for the so-called "Northern Lights Wall", and during construction a third version was actualised. The final drawings were completed before and after the Aalto couple's first trip to America. Aalto used his beloved Aurora Borealis Wall in a miniaturised form at the beginning of the 1970s for the museum building named after him.

Axonometric projection

Left page:
The large interior space with the "Northern Lights Wall"

Unfolding of the themed wall

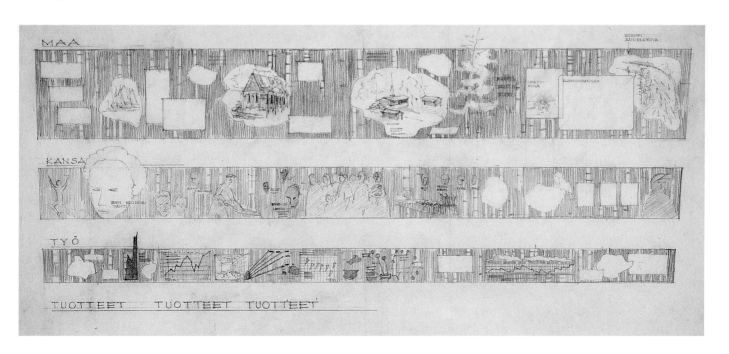

1947–1949 ▸ "Baker House"
Student Dormitory, Massachusetts Institute of Technology ▸ Cambridge, Massachusetts

Left page:
View of the river side

Student room

In 1940 Aalto was appointed Research Fellow at MIT. In 1945, after the war, he went back to Cambridge to teach, at the invitation of architect and new deacon of the university, his old friend William W. Wurster. In this context Aalto was commissioned in 1946 to plan a new student dormitory. The building plans were drawn up at the end of 1947 in collaboration with the local architectural firm Parry, Shaw & Hepburn, and shortly afterward the construction was begun. Aino Aalto died at the beginning of 1949. The opening of the dormitory took place under these sorrowful circumstances.

The student dormitory is located on the urban campus of MIT, on the shore of Charles River. The main traffic artery of the region, Memorial Drive, runs between the buildings and the river, and thus one could not exactly call the location ideal. Because of the budgetary situation aggravated by the war and the performance-focused mentality that resulted, the cost calculations for the dormitory were based on a per-bed price, which forced Aalto to maximise the number of rooms in relation to the number of square metres. Single-person rooms make up the majority, but there are two-bed and three-bed rooms in the building as well. Aalto took pains to find a solution for the problem of the restless surroundings and optimised living by designing the southern façade to open up to the river like an arch. The windows of the flats open to the south,

Campus façade with main entrance

to the natural light and to the river landscape, and thus all of the windows are at an angle to the street, meaning that one can follow the traffic zooming by as pleasantly as possible, exactly like one follows the landscape rushing by from a moving train best by looking at it from the window at a slanted perspective. Aalto wanted to provide the main façade of the residential section with a trellis covered by thick ivy. A roof garden was planned as well. Yet these solutions, which were intended to bring the residential surroundings closer to the natural environment, were dropped due to financial reasons.

The idea behind the planning of the student dormitory is crystallised in the following quote from Aalto: "We can formulate the ideal goal of architecture by saying that it is the purpose of a building to be an instrument that collects all of nature's positive forces for the resident; on the other hand architecture has the duty to protect the resident from all of the unfavourable forces that occur in nature and in the building's surroundings."

Irregularly burned bricks were used as material for the façade. Aalto insisted furthermore on the use of scrap material walled in such way that the altered parts protrude over the smooth surface, thus giving the surface a desired irregularity. The top six storeys of the seven-storey dormitory wing are storey-wide flats. Aalto took pains to house the function rooms and the hallways of these floors on the north side of the

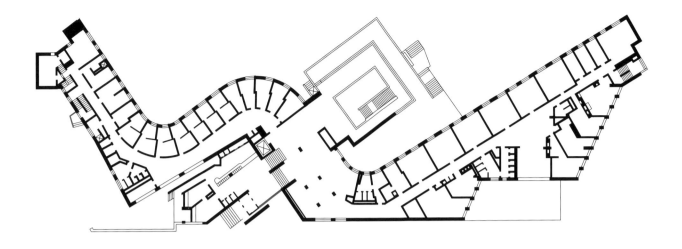

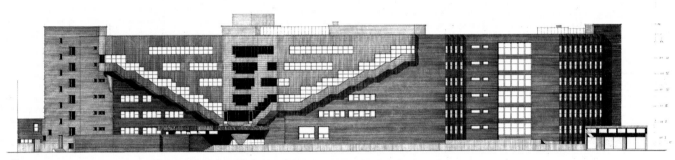

building. The projecting, single-flight stairwells form a dominant wedge on the north façade. The combination of a soft wave form and sharp-edged projections gives the two sides of the building a startling contrast.

A canteen and a café are housed in a separate wing between the dormitory building and the river. In contrast to the other buildings, the low, rectangular restaurant wing has grey marble as façade material. The canteen rooms are brightened by round skylights, characteristic of Aalto's architecture.

As a result of the organic form of the façade, the rooms vary in form, whereby the use of standard furnishing solutions was restricted. The top-quality furnishing was planned by Aino Aalto. The furniture was provided by Svenska Artek, and the built-in fixtures were from the local manufacturer Cory.

Above:
Plan

Below:
Elevation

1949–1952 ▸ Säynätsalo Town Hall
Jyväskylä, Finland

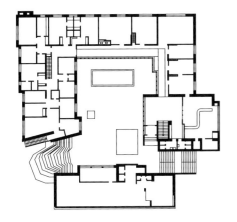

Floor plan

Left page:
View from the street

Many ideals and ideas in Alvar Aalto's architecture originate from the Mediterranean countries. The citizens' forum, as a democratic and symbolic gathering place, plays a significant role in almost all of the city centres that Aalto planned. A new avowal to monumentality came with this, having been frowned upon for a long time under the dictation of functionalism.

Alvar Aalto created his construction plan for Säynätsalo, the small industrial town of 3,000 inhabitants, from 1942 to 1947. Even then he had sketched the town centre as an open square. A new administrative building was to stand on one side of the square. At Aalto's recommendation, a planning competition for the town hall was announced in 1949, which he then won under the pseudonym "Curia". The construction began in the spring of 1950 and the town hall was completed in 1952.

The town hall does not just have a purely administrative function, but also houses business and residential rooms. In addition to the district council conference hall and the office rooms, plans were made for a library, a pharmacy, a bank, more business rooms, flats and a sauna as well. The town hall was supposed to have three storeys in accordance with the guidelines, but in Aalto's plan only the conference hall is higher than two storeys. The floor space of the town hall adds up to about 1,800 square metres.

Stairs covered with greenery to the interior courtyard

Above:
View of the interior courtyard

Right:
Competition entry

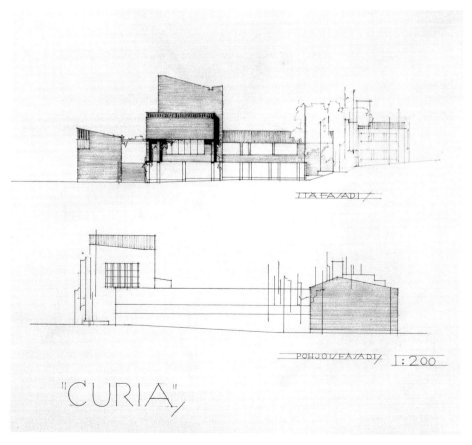

Town Hall Council Chamber

Alvar Aalto paraphrases the idea as such: "This construction, which stands on a relatively steep slope, is built with its single and double storey sections around the central courtyard, the patio. The interior courtyard forms a raised surface, which arose when the soil that was left over during the foundation excavation was used directly for this raising. Offices were envisioned for the ground floor. The actual administrative building, whose rooms were grouped around the patio, was freed from the vulgarising effect of the businesses by building two levels, a street level and a patio level." One gets to the raised interior courtyard via the granite main stairs on the east corner or via the grassy stairs on the west side.

The predominant material of the town hall for the exterior as well as in the public rooms is unplastered red brick. A tower-like rising mass dominates the architecture of the house. Aalto: "One of the most important duties of architecture is to find the right scale. The Säynätsalo Town Hall, with its small central square and its location at the last point of the wedge-shaped central marketplace, is an attempt in this direction. The various parts of the building all act in pursuance to their own scale. The tower is not a tower, but rather a unifying mass that covers the council hall, or the main symbol of the administration, that lies below it."

Plenty of wood was used in the interior rooms and the furnishing designed by Aalto. In the council hall the low amount of light from the north is filtered in by a window covered with slats. The ceiling is dominated by two butterfly-like wooden trusses that render air exchange between the ceiling and the roof possible.

In spite of its small size, the Säynätsalo Town Hall has a rare monumentality. Aalto avoided everything decorative; he elevated simple and reduced materials and a discreet scale to the main characteristic of his architecture. He once compared his town hall to the Palazzo Pubblico of Siena, which he considered to be one of the most beautiful achievements of European urban culture. Both have a similar duty to unify and symbolise democratic values.

The Säynätsalo Town Hall introduced a new period in Aalto's creation, typified by the use of red brick, wood, copper and other natural materials as well as by a reduced language of forms. The town hall counts as one of the most significant of Aalto's buildings. It was classified as a historical monument in 1994.

Door handle on the town hall entrance

1949–1974 · Institute of Technology
Espoo, Finland

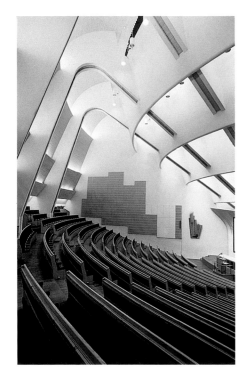

Large lecture hall

Left page:
Large lecture hall, seen from the west

The campus of the Helsinki Institute of Technology is located north-west of the city centre, in the Otaniemi district of the neighbouring city Espoo. In 1949 Aalto won the planning competition for the overall plan with his suggestion "Ave Alma Mater morituri te salutant". The schematic competition entry formed the basis for future planning and additions. It envisions the construction of the central university building on a hill in the middle of the campus. In addition the plan contains a dormitory for the students and a residential development on the seashore for the teaching faculty, with single-family homes for the professors and flats in small residential buildings for the rest of the personnel.

Aalto brought the Anglo-Saxon notion of a campus to Finland with his competition entry for the Institute of Technology. In 1949 he had just returned to Finland from the United States and had been influenced by American university culture.

The campus is located in park-like surroundings; its centre is made up of a grouping of buildings around the central square, containing the main building as well as teaching buildings and laboratories. The rooms of the general department and of the geodesy and architecture faculties are connected to the main building. It was planned to house the other faculties in further buildings. The actual planning work began in 1953, and the plans for the main building were completed in 1955. Construction was not begun until 1962, and the main building was inaugurated on the 1st of September 1966. The furnishing work lasted until the following year.

As shown in the plan, the main building is situated on a hill and is connected with the other building groups in a complex structure. In the centre is the auditorium, which, when seen from the outside, forms a sloped cylindrical segment, which rises in a funnel shape over the building compound. Seen from the side of the court, it serves as an outdoor theatre. The interior of the auditorium is dominated by the expressive concrete construction, emphasised by the natural light streaming inside through the skylights.

The main entrance is situated in the base of the auditorium. The administrative section is located north of the tower-like middle. A rectangular lecture room and a hall are on the first storey, and a café for the teaching staff and the students is on the ground floor. To the east of the main entrance, there are groups of buildings extending along an east-west axis with seminar rooms connected by a central corridor. These wings range from being one storey to four storeys high, and there are small yards between the rows. To the south, the architecture faculty is in the last building, having thus received special placement in the building hierarchy.

The predominant materials of the buildings are specially manufactured red bricks, black granite and copper. The complex was planned with future additions in mind; the main building was expanded upon for the first time between 1966 and 1977. Other buildings designed by Aalto that belonged to his overall plan were realised next to the main building. This includes Otahalli, a gymnasium in the southern part of Otaniemi that was completed from 1949 to 1952, right after the competition. It is a wooden-

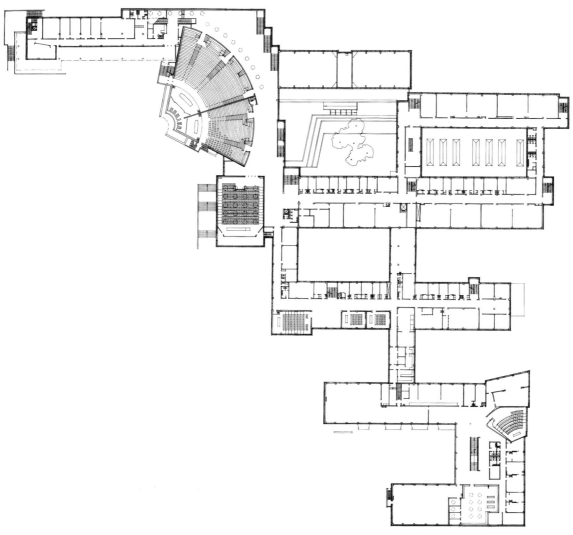

Institute building

Left page:
Complete view from south

Suspended lamp

Left page:
Floor plan

arched construction, advanced for its time, with a staggered wall surface that follows the oval of the race track, with large windows in the upper section.

The central library with its café and library rooms is located on the west edge of the central square and separates the pedestrian area from the street area. It was conceived as a counterpart to the main building and was completed between 1964 and 1969.

In 1950 Aalto participated in a competition to plan a shopping mall and student dormitories for the settlement. On the basis of his plans, the banking and business building was built from 1960 to 1961, and the dormitory was built from 1962 to 1966. The lengthy shopping mall, with its copper roof, stands on the southern edge of the central square on a sloping site. Business rooms are located on both sides of the single-storey building. The student dormitory, used during the summer as a hotel, is located on the south-eastern part of the site. Here Aalto combined rectangular buildings with a fan-shaped room layout, as he had already done for the dormitory at MIT, where wedge-shaped rooms had made a curved façade possible. The entrance courtyard is between these building wings with their different characters. The hallways on the floors function as social rooms; in a manner typical for collective student living, the dwelling units have a common kitchen and a common living room.

It was the starting point of the entire plan to leave possibilities for additions open for future needs. In the meantime, many buildings from other Finnish architects have been added. In 1962 and 1963 a heating plant designed by Aalto was built to the northeast. In this red brick building, rooms for the needs of technical instruction and research are also integrated. In a manner typical for Aalto's industrial buildings, the large window panes bring light into the interior rooms and open up a view of the inside to passers-by.

1951–1959 ⋅ Pedagogical University
Jyväskylä, Finland

Canteen

Left page:
View of the interior courtyard

Aalto won the architecture competition for the Jyväskylä Pedagogical University in 1951 with his suggestion "Urbs". Since he had grown up here, he dedicated himself to this project with special devotion.

The University of Jyväskylä campus is located in a hilly landscape immediately south of the city centre at the end of a ridge that divides the city. This area had seminar buildings built of red brick dating back from the 1880s. Aalto oriented himself to this continuance and carried it on to this modern campus by using red bricks in his buildings as well. Aalto divided the campus from the centre of the city and grouped the buildings in horseshoe form around a sports field. A footpath leads from Kauppakatu Street, the main street of the centre, at a slanted angle to the main building of the university and connects the campus with the city in this way. When one leaves the centre, the main building acts as the façade of the university, and the other buildings are located behind it in park-like territory.

During the first construction phase from 1952 to 1953 the practice school, a sports hall, the canteens Lozzi and Lyhty, the dormitory and the heating plant were completed. During the second construction phase from 1954 to 1955, a second sports hall, the residential building for the personnel, an indoor swimming pool, the main building and the library were built.

The main building is made up of a ballroom, an administrative wing and a connecting stairwell hall. The façade of the building, divided into three parts, is a reply to the form of the ballroom on the upper level. This ballroom can be divided in the middle. The foyer on the ground floor opens to the surrounding nature through glass walls. An open square is in front of the entrance side of the main building, from which one can see

Handrail detail

the landscape around Jyväsjärvi Lake to the east. Behind the main building, on the south side, there is a small graduated square which can be used for outdoor performances.

The canteen and dormitory building east of the sports field is laid out on the sloping site in terraces. The west side of the sports field is dominated by a long bar formed by two gymnasiums and an indoor swimming pool between them. Aalto planned two urbanistic perspectives for the campus: one of the main square, when one comes from the centre, and the second from the sports field onto the interior of the horseshoe-shaped ensemble.

After this Aalto planned the students' house and the sports faculty. The buildings with their various functions form a closed whole in which the individual buildings connect to each other to form spacious room complexes. Besides red brick, Aalto also used wood, glass and granite, and in the interior rooms marble, ceramic and high-grade wood types were used. The campus complex on Seminaarinmäki Hill has been under monument protection since 1992. This university campus, which from its inception has been planned with the possibility of additions in mind, has been extended several times south-eastward.

Entrance front on the city side

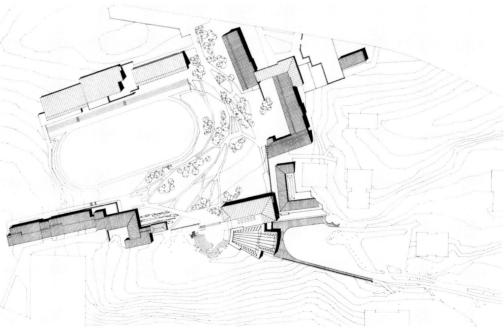

Site plan

1951–1987 ▸ Town Centre
Seinäjoki, Finland

Town hall and streetlight

The town of Seinäjoki lies in East Bothnia, where Lutheran religious communities have traditionally had a strong social significance. The centre of Seinäjoki, which reflects the Anglo-American "Civic Centre" ideology, is Aalto's most consistently realised town centre plan.

In 1951, the Seinäjoki church parish announced a competition for the construction of a church and a parish centre. Aalto participated in the competition with his proposal "Lakeuden risti" (Cross of the Plains). He envisioned a free square in front of the entrance façade of the church in which religious events could take place in the summer. The square was created sloping toward the church with the parish rooms grouped in low buildings around it. Aalto's design, which diverged markedly from the other contributions, exceeded the predetermined building limits by some ten metres and thus could not be awarded due to its disregard of the competition provisions. Yet the jury selected Aalto's proposal in spite of this and recommended it as the basis for the realisation.

In 1956 Aalto was commissioned to develop the plan further. The church was built between 1958 and 1960 and the parish centre from 1964 to 1966. For financial reasons, the plan for a black granite façade had to be substituted with white-rendered brick. As a compromise, the side chapel was layered with black granite. On the northern edge of the site, a 65 metre high bell tower in the form of a stylised cross was erected, visible from afar.

The church has 1,400 seats; the church hall is a wedge-shaped, symmetrical room that becomes slightly narrower toward the altar. A small chapel for baptisms and weddings is located between the sacristy and the bell tower. A straight axis leads from the main entry door to the central square across from it which was built later and is now used as an outdoor church. The adjacent low parish hall is divided by stairs that lead to the square. Aalto even designed the church textiles and the models of the Last Supper.

In 1958 the Seinäjoki town council announced two competitions to design a new centre, envisioned to be very close to the church. Aalto did not win the competition this time either, once again due to an technical error, but was again commissioned with the planning. The first competition applied to the entire area, the second to the town hall. Aalto took part in the latter competition with his proposal "Kaupungitalo A" (Town Hall A). Aalto envisioned a continuation of the series of rooms formed by open squares, to be attached to the church and the community centre. The first open square is the lawn in front of the church, the second is the central citizens' square, also reserved for pedestrians, and the third is a star-shaped intersection west of the centre. The complete town centre, including the property works, fountains and the paving of the sidewalks, was only built little by little.

The town hall was built from 1963–1965 diagonally across from the church complex, north of the citizens' square. The S-shaped town hall, like the parish district, is located partly on an artificial hill that resulted during the excavation of the foundation. On the main entrance side, the council hall, which opens toward the church, was

Left page:
Town hall and church

Municipal library

Right page, top:
View of the town hall from the theatre café

Right page, bottom:
Site plan

raised to the level of the first storey using columns. From the other side of the council hall one arrives at an interior courtyard on a hill, which slopes down in terraces to the citizens' square. On the north side, the office wing separates the yard from the street. The council has a rectangular floor plan; the chairman's seat is located in a corner, and the seats of the delegates are arranged in three wedge-shaped sectors. The benches for the audience were planned to be at the same level as the delegates.

In his competition entry Aalto had chosen a space on the south side of the citizens' square for the library. When he was putting the finishing touches on the plans from 1960 to 1965, he changed the form. Instead of the planned rectangular building with a wedge-shaped book repository on the south side and an auditorium against a front wall, there was now an elongated building with a fan-shaped lending and books hall pushing forward out of its front façade. In the middle of the asymmetrical hall are the lending and supervisory desks and an open reading hall a few steps lower. The lending desk and this lower-level reading hall are encircled by a row of columns supporting the ceiling. The large windows are directed southward toward the light. Horizontal lamellae are mounted outside onto the window wall that are intended to prevent direct light from intruding. The children's section, the manuals section, the assembly rooms and offices are located on both sides of the main hall. The whitewashed library was inaugurated in 1965.

The low, public administrative building stands at the end of the axis that begins at the church and crosses the citizens' square. This three-storey building borders the centre to the west. The plans for the town theatre remained largely as they had been in the competition entry, and the location was kept as well. The final version of the theatre, which is located between the library and the administrative building, was sketched by his office under the leadership of Elissa Aalto from 1984 to 1987, after Alvar Aalto's death.

Stained-glass windows of the church designed by Aalto

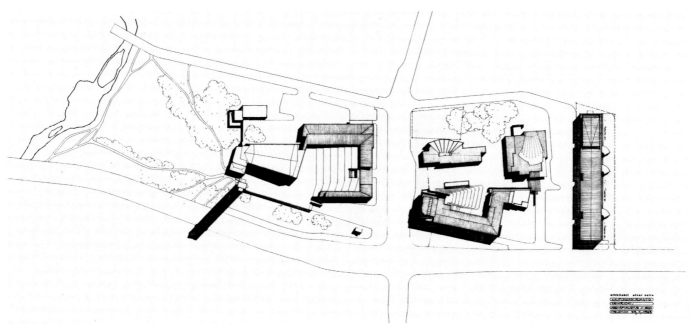

1952–1954 ▸ Experimental Summer House
Muuratsalo, Finland

The summer house in Muuratsalo was an important piece of architecture for Alvar Aalto. His first wife, Aino, had died in 1949. The plans for the Säynätsalo Town Hall had begun in the same year, and the young architect Elsa (later Elissa) Mäkiniemi had joined the Aalto Office. During the construction on the town hall Alvar and Elissa found a scenic plot of land on the nearby island of Muuratsalo, where in 1952, after their marriage, they built themselves a summer house, or as Aalto called it, an experimental laboratory.

Aalto was already familiar with the area around Muuratsalo, as his parents had moved from the lowlands of western Finland to Jyväskylä at the turn of the century, in 1903. The landscape inland is dominated by lakes and forested hills. The culture of summer houses and boats had a high significance for the life of the educated classes in the small town.

The house is located directly on a rock that rises up out of the water. Both the scale and the many technical solutions are oriented to the conditions of the surrounding nature. The foundations, for example, rest on natural rock. The section from the first phase of construction, made of brick, is muddled white on the exterior. The guest wing, which was built a year later, is built of wood and painted white, and rises up onto a forested slope. The construction has a heroic location that is reminiscent of the nature-oriented Greek temples.

Site plan

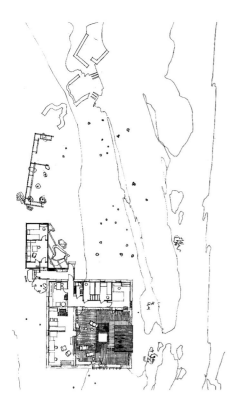

In contrast to the white exterior wall, the walls of the interior courtyard predominantly consist of red brick. Fifty different types of brick were used for this in order to test out their respective durability and their optical effect. The rooms of the main section are grouped around the interior court. An open fireplace is in the middle. The living room and the studio are located in the northern part on the gallery, and the bedrooms are in the east part. The kitchen and the sanitary facilities are housed in the connecting section; from here one reaches the guest wing by means of an ingeniously worked out hallway.

In the summer house one can discover many central elements of Aalto's architecture. The interior courtyard is a good example of the elegant and delicate way in which he frequently disrupted the boundary between the interior and the exterior. The view from the living space opens up to the lake. From the window of the bedroom one can see out over the yard and through an opening in the wall to the tower of the Church of Muurame, which Aalto designed in the 1920s. The house has both romantic and archaic traits. Free-standing walls and openings suggest something past and lost; in this lies the nostalgia of ruins. The relationship of the building to nature appears almost mythical. Aalto wrote in 1921: "Nothing old is born anew. Yet it doesn't disappear completely either. And what has already been arises again and again in new form."

The Villa Mairea and the summer house have experimentation and the "game" in common, each in a positive way. Both houses were a kind of experimental laboratory for Aalto, a means to develop architecture further and improve it.

Above:
Interior court with fireplace in the middle

Right:
View from the living room into the court

Living room
Aalto used the higher-lying area as a painting
studio.

Motorboat "Nemo propheta in patria", 1954

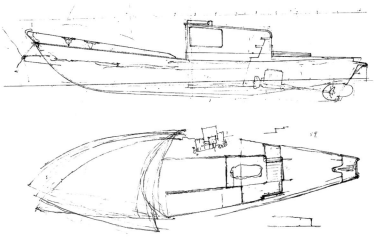

1952–1958 ▸ "House of Culture"
Sturenkatu, Helsinki, Finland

In 1952 the Communist Party of Finland turned to Aalto and asked him to plan a building complex in Helsinki. Aalto agreed, and the company "Helsinki House of Culture" was founded in order to carry out the construction. The edifice encompassed the headquarters of the Party, club rooms and a cultural centre. The site is located in the historically blue-collar district Alppila, on the Alppiharju cliffs on much-travelled Sturenkatu Street. The cultural centre was mostly constructed by volunteer community teamwork. It was opened in 1958.

Aalto considered various alternatives during initial planning to satisfy the required space for the political, cultural, social and administrative purposes. Especially the sizeable height differences of the site made the planning a challenge.

The final layout of the ground plan in a U-shape was not decided on until the end of the planning phase. According to the construction design, Aalto's plan envisaged a three part complex. He put the large, brick, free-standing auditorium section and the rectangular five-storey office wing with a copper roof next to each other on the street. They are connected in the rear area by a low section, making the space between the buildings a courtyard.

The office wing originally had one hundred ten rooms. A hall, the wardrobe, a lecture hall, three classrooms, five assembly rooms, the library and a gymnasium were located in the connecting section on the basement level. The main rooms of the auditorium were the congress hall and the concert hall for 1,500 people with a restaurant, as well as a small cinema auditorium in the basement. Both wings of the complex are connected on Sturenkatu Street by a sixty metre long roofing which serves as a gate to the courtyard. The sculpture "The Builder's Hand" by Wäinö Aaltonen stands in the middle of the sparkling spring fountain in the courtyard, symbolising the work of the volunteers.

The fundamental idea of the MIT student dormitory, completed nearly ten years before, is diversified here by the use of red bricks and the combination of free and angular form. The central idea of the House of Culture becomes clear in the asymmetrical auditorium. Aalto developed a wedge-shaped brick for the waved exterior wall. The lively form of this brick wall represents Aalto's ambition for an organic architecture in nuance-rich form.

View from the street

Right:
Section model

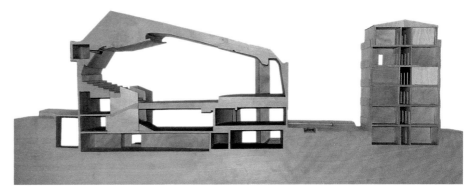

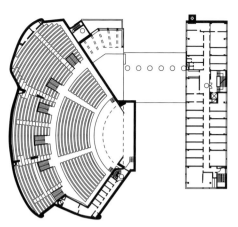

Plan

Left:
View from the street

Right page:
Interior court with fountain

Below:
Handrail detail

Aalto further developed his ideas on acoustically optimal ceiling surfaces and wall surfaces in this auditorium with its especially broad appearance. Hence, this auditorium, famous for its acoustics, has often been used by orchestras for recordings. In 1989 the building was classified as a historical monument and in 1990 and 1991 respectfully renovated from the ground up. In this context the Communist Party sold the building. Today the Radio Symphony Orchestra and the architectural history department of the Museum Office are housed in its rooms.

1955–1957 ‣ Hansaviertel Block of Flats
Berlin, Germany

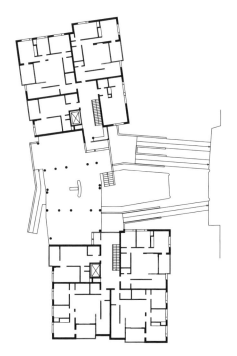

Top left:
Ground floor plan

Top right:
Flat model

Below:
Ceiling painting on the ground floor

Left page:
Exterior view

In 1957, the large international exhibition Interbau took place in Berlin. The theme of the exhibition for urban construction was "The City of Tomorrow". This name indicates trends typical for that time as well as its faith in the future. In 1955, Aalto and 52 other internationally-known architects were commissioned to plan blocks of flats, to be realised approximately six kilometres away from the centre of Berlin in the Hansa-viertel, quarter of the Tiergarten district. Other significant planners of this modern residential quarter were Walter Gropius and Oscar Niemeyer, among others.

The eight-storey building designed by Aalto accommodates 78 flats. One of the flats was furnished for the duration of the exhibition; this furniture had been designed for an exhibition in Helsingborg, Sweden.

According to Aalto's plan, the rectangular flats of various sizes are grouped around two stairwells next to each other. The ground floor is open between the stairwells in the middle. In this way it forms both a connection between the front and rear yards as well as a roofed entrance area.

In his Hansaviertel Block of Flats, one can discover several characteristics that emphasise community as well as privacy, typical for Aalto's later blocks of flats: for example, the bright stairwells and the closed, pulled-in balconies. The function of the balconies is to form a natural transition between the interior and the exterior, bringing the outside into the flat.

1955–1958 · Church of the Three Crosses
Vuoksenniska, Imatra, Finland

The industrial town of Imatra lies in eastern Finland, in the Saimaa lake district. In 1955 Aalto began with the planning of the church, which was built in 1958 at a relatively secluded location, as an extension of the completed Imatra master plan.

The church in Vuoksenniska is regarded as Aalto's most original church building. Aalto chose the conflict between the religious and the practical functions of the church as an ambitious starting point for his planning. He recognised the special social function of the church in an industrial area and realised that the parish rooms, with their social emphasis, had usurped the actual church buildings' character as public monuments.

Aalto solved this problem by connecting the essential club rooms, parish halls and the actual church room to a room that could be separated if needed, formed by three church halls in succession. The hall at the north-western end, in which the altar is located, is the actual sanctuary.

The other two rooms can be separated by movable partition walls if necessary. The walls, which can be moved by electric motors, have a thickness of forty-two centimetres and are fully soundproof. On weekdays, these two halls, each of which has over three hundred seats, are used for congregational purposes. The church has altogether six entrances so that the three sections can be used independently from each other as smoothly as possible. The hall can be used as a mourning chapel, and from it one arrives through a door directly to the cemetery, located in a pine grove. Two more function-rooms and a morgue are located in the basement. Altogether the church has more than eight hundred seats.

The walls are partly straight and partly curved due to acoustic reasons, according to Aalto. Lutheran church services require three central points for every church hall: altar, pulpit and organ loft, where the choir often stands. According to Aalto's solution the partition walls diagonally across from the pulpit have a curved form; they cut off the corner of the hall furthest away from the pulpit. Thus, during the sermon, churchgoers all sit about the same distance away from the pulpit. The organ loft is located to the right of the altar above the entrance. During the planning of the acoustics of the interior a miniature model was used with mirrors reflecting rays of light, intended to make the sound waves visible.

The division of the interior into three sections is repeated as a theological motif in the three crosses of the altar. The official name of the church is "Church of the Three Crosses". The south-western wall is the main window wall of the church; the windows are placed high. Of the one hundred three window panes, only two have the same form. The plastic forms of the interior mask the supporting construction; the interior and exterior are independent of each other in form.

The interior and exterior walls of the north-eastern façade, between which one can slide the curved partition walls, differ in their construction from the other walls, exactly as the forty-three metre high bell tower of reinforced concrete, the top point of which ends in plastic. With this solution Aalto wanted to highlight the white church tower as a symbol between the factory chimneys.

The prevailing colour of the church is white. The façade is made of whitewashed brick and concrete. The interior is completely white, with the exception of the lead glass window. Aalto designed it himself, and its theme is the crown of thorns. The church textiles were designed by the artist Greta Skogster-Lehtinen. The low-sloping dark copper roof on the south-eastern end creates a contrast to the general brightness.

A single-storey parsonage with a wavy ridge stands next to the church, in which the flats for pastors and staff of the church are located. A white concrete wall connects the building with the church and encloses a sheltered yard.

1956–1961 ▸ Maison Carré
Bazoches-sur-Guyonne, France

Left page:
Entrance hall with curved pinewood ceiling

The French gallery owner Louis Carré (1897–1977) and Alvar Aalto belonged to the same generation and had numerous artist friends in common, for example Fernand Léger and Alexander Calder. Yet they met each other for the first time in the summer of 1956 in Venice, when Aalto's pavilion was opened at the Biennale. The reason for their meeting was Louis Carré's wish to have Aalto plan his new house. The spark between the two was immediate, and it was to become a life-long friendship.

In the year prior, Louis Carré had acquired quite a large plot of land in the small village of Bazoches-sur-Guyonne between Chartres and Versailles, just under 50 kilometres away from Paris. He and his wife Olga intended to move into the new home permanently. It was supposed to be a house for both private life as well as representation and meetings with customers. How best to present artwork and jewels was supposed to be considered during the planning, as well as the library, which was of special importance to Louis Carré. In addition to these wishes, Louis Carré had an idea of a house "small from the outside yet big from the inside" and with an architecturally significant roof. Aalto was given a free hand to plan the rest, which he began with enthusiasm as soon as the fall of the same year. The Carré couple moved into the house in July of 1959. A swimming pool and a dressing room were completed in 1963.

The starting point of the plans for the Maison Carré was similar to that of the Villa Mairea two decades prior. Whereas the Villa Mairea stands in a Finnish pine forest, the Maison Carré has a vast rural landscape opening up around it. Here again Aalto's plan did not just apply to the building. Aalto envisioned a small vineyard by the house, and similar to the Säynätsalo Town Hall, he terraced the slope to the forest, stabilising it with vertically split tree trunks. At the lower edge of the site he planned a small theatre stage reminiscent of the solution at the site of his own office building from 1955.

The appearance of the Maison Carré is dominated by the protruding pent roof that reflects the shape of the surrounding landscape. Aalto discovered the blue-black slate found in the region, from which 600 x 300 x 7 millimetre slabs were made to measure. The base and the paving were made of limestone from Chartres. For the rest, mainly whitewashed brick and, in some places, marble as well were used as wall material. The timber structures on the exterior are painted white. The entrance hall has an almost sacral appearance, dominated by a wavy ceiling made of red pine wood from Finnish Lapland. One can see vague similarities to the ceiling of the Viipuri Municipal Library

Side section

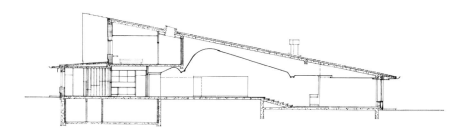

View from the outside

in it. The walls and the lighting are conceived for the presentation of works of art. A wide stairway leads down to a living room; according to Aalto, the scale is the same as that of stairs in Versailles. The room is dominated by a tiered wooden ceiling and wide windows that open up to the garden. The study is located to the right, Louis Carré's library. Finnish carpenters were commissioned with the woodwork of the interior.

The bedrooms of Olga and Louis Carré as well as a guest room are located behind the light walls of the entrance hall that divide the room. There is a small sauna that is connected to Louis Carré's bedroom, and from there one can reach a sheltered place in the garden. The dining hall, kitchen and utility rooms lie to the side facing the slope. The four rooms for the house staff are located on the upper storey of the house.

The rich world of details designed by Aalto forms the counterbalance to the large, elegant curves of the Maison Carré. The altogether nearly two hundred individual elements, such as door handles, wall units, lights and furniture, make the house a synthesis of several art forms. The Maison Carré has been classified as a historical monument since 1996.

Ground floor plan

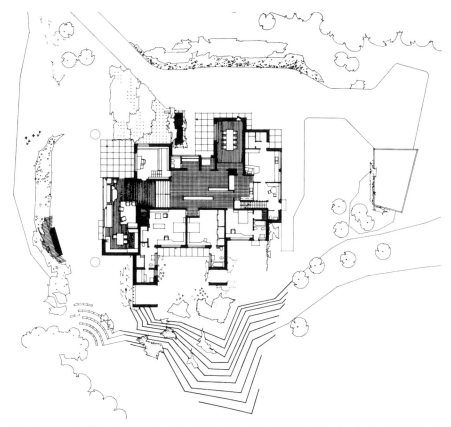

Living room

1958–1962 ‣ Neue Vahr Block of Flats
Bremen, Germany

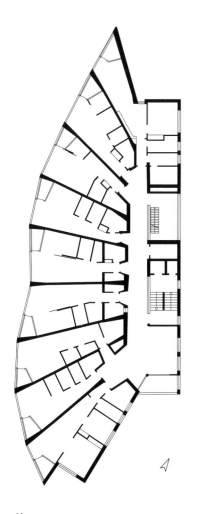

Between 1958 and 1962, Aalto planned a twenty-two storey block of flats in Bremen. The building stands in a suburb directly next to a large park. The non-profit housing association GEWOBA had the building erected as a landmark of the social model construction area Neue Vahr. Every floor of the building, made of bitumen-treated concrete elements, has nine single or double room flatlets.

Aalto tried out various forms as early as the sketching stage. The flats have roomy living rooms that open up to the west. The living rooms have a large window and a balcony next to it that is flush with the façade. The fan-shaped form of the mostly closed balconies protect the private sphere.

The building was meant for social-collective living following the ideals of Scandinavian modernity, which is why every storey has a communal room. Here Aalto left it up to the "imagination of the future inhabitants and the building firm ... whether these twenty communal rooms should be designed with sitting corners, deckchairs, game facilities, reading and writing closets or table tennis facilities". The elevators, the stairwell and the ventilation balconies are located on the east side of the building. On the top storey there are club rooms and a roofed look-out terrace. The ground floor has rooms for offices and small stores instead of flats. Pedestrians have direct access to the central square of the estate and to the car park.

Above:
Floor plan

Right:
One of the slant-angled living rooms

Left page:
View from the east

1962–1975 ▸ Finlandia Hall
Helsinki, Finland

Section

Left page:
Auditorium

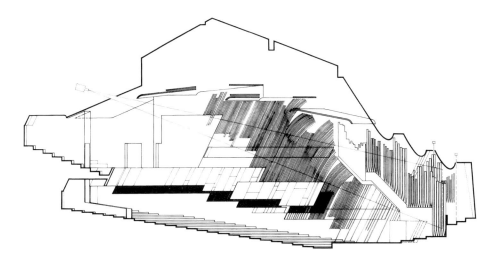

Bayside

In 1962 the city of Helsinki commissioned Alvar Aalto to plan a concert and congress hall, the first part of his big plan for the city centre. The main traits of the final version are already visible in the first designs from the year 1967. Later, the structure of the façade and the chamber music hall were changed.

The eastern main façade opens up to Töölö Bay. The actual entrance is located on the first storey of the side facing the park. It leads into the entrance hall, in which the cloakroom and various service rooms are located. The wide "Venetian stairway" leads to the foyer, from which one comes to the large hall, the small hall or the restaurant. Two smaller stairways lead out of the foyer into a type of gallery, from which one arrives at the tier of the large hall. The small chamber music hall has 350 seats, and the large hall has 1,750.

Aalto varied a few of the main ideas of his opera house in Essen for the Finlandia Hall. This helped him get over the delay of the German project. Yet this was to prove to be a blessing. When the construction began in Essen in 1987, two solutions could be avoided that had proved to be problematic for the Finlandia Hall: the use of the brittle Carrara marble for the façades and the large room as a "sounding body", intended to be a regulator of the acoustics.

The Finlandia Hall was opened in 1971, and in 1975 the congress wing was completed. This connects to the main building on the south side. It contains a large foyer, assembly rooms of various sizes and two large congress halls which can be combined to form one room for nine hundred people. Large windows and concave recesses are on the western façade, serving to protect the old trees of the site and to enliven the façade.

Life and Work

1898 ▶ Hugo Alvar Henrik Aalto is born on 3 February in Kuortane, in the Grand Principality of Finland, part of the Tsarist Empire.

1903 ▶ The Aalto family relocates to Jyväskylä.

1906 ▶ Alvar Aalto's mother dies.

1907 ▶ His father and his mother's sister, Flora, get married.

1916 ▶ Alvar passes the matriculation examination. After work experience during the summer under the direction of the architect Salervo, he travels in the fall by steamboat to Helsinki, where he begins his studies at the Technical University.

1918 ▶ His studies are interrupted by the civil war. Alvar takes part in the war in the rows of the conservative "Whites". The Aalto family relocates to Alajärvi. Aalto is commissioned by his father to reconstruct the house Mammula, Aalto's first realised project.

1921 ▶ Aalto finishes his architecture studies and receives the grade "laudable" for his dissertation. He becomes a member of the newly-founded Finnish Association of Architects, SAFA.

1923 ▶ Aalto moves to Jyväskylä and establishes his first architectural office.
Villa Manner, Töysä

1924 ▶ The architect Aino Marsio (Mandelin) and Alvar Aalto are married on 6 October.
Workers' Club and Theatre, Jyväskylä
Aira Apartment Building, Jyväskylä
Defence Corps Building, Seinäjoki

1925 ▶ "A beautification measure in our city and its possibilities" appears in the local newspaper, an important statement of Aalto. A daughter, Johanna (Hanni) is born.

1926
Defence Corps Building, Jyväskylä
Church, Muurame

1927 ▶ Move to Turku.

Agriculture Cooperative Building, Turku
Standard apartment house, Turku
Library, Viipuri (now Russia)

1928 ▶ The couple goes on a study-trip to Central Europe. A son, Hamilkar, is born.
Turun Sanomat Newspaper Offices, Turku
Tuberkulosis Sanatorium, Paimio

1932 ▶ Aino receives the second prize at a functional glass competition of the glass factory Karhula-Iittala. Alvar's proposal is realised.
Villa Tammekann, Tarto, Estonia

1933 ▶ The Aalto couple moves to Helsinki. Exhibition of the couple's furniture in London and Milan.

1934 ▶ Furniture exhibition in Helsinki and Zurich.

Alvar Aalto in the 1940s at his workdesk

Left Page:
Aalto around 1965

1935 ▶ The Aalto couple founds the Artek Company with Maire Gullichsen and Nils Gustav Hahl.
Aalto House on Riihitie, Helsinki

1936 ▶ The Aalto couple moves into their new home and office on the Riihitie. They take part in the design exhibition in Milan and in Paris.
Finnish Pavilion, Paris World's Fair
Cellulose Factory and Housing Area, Sunila, Kotka
Savoy restaurant interior, Helsinki

1937
Art museum, competition entry, Tallinn, Estonia
Terraced house type, Kauttua, Eura

1938 ▶ The Aalto couple travels to the United States for the first time.
Villa Mairea, Noormarkku
Finnish Pavilion, New York World's Fair
Elementary school, Inkeroinen

1940 ▶ Alvar travels with his family to Washington and is appointed as a professor at MIT. Return to Finland in the middle of war.

1941 ▶ Aalto gives a lecture in Switzerland about reconstruction.
Regional Plan for the Kokemäenjoki Valley, Kokemäki

1943 ▶ Aalto is elected chairman of the Association of Architects and travels with a delegation to Germany.

1944 ▶ Aalto takes part in the exhibition "Vi bor i Friluftstaden" in Sweden and organises the exhibition "Amerikka rakentaa" in Helsinki.

1945–1946 ▶ Professorship in the United States.

1947 ▶ Exhibition on the occasion of the 25th anniversary of the cooperation between Aino and Alvar Aalto in the Helsinki Art Hall. From there the exhibition travels to several European countries.
MIT Student Dormitory, Cambridge, Massachusetts, USA

1948 ▶ Aalto ends his teaching at MIT and returns to Finland because of Aino's grave sickness.

1949 ▸ Aino Aalto dies on 13 January.
Institute of Technology, Otaniemi, Espoo
Town Hall, Säynätsalo

1950
Malmi Funeral Chapel (competition entry),
Helsinki

1951
Rautatalo Office Building, Helsinki
Church "Lakeuden risti" (Cross of the Plains),
Seinäjoki
Institute of Pedagogics (now University), Jyväskylä

1952 ▸ The architect Elissa (Elsa) Mäkiniemi and
Alvar are married on 4 October.
Experimental Summer House, Muuratsalo
"House of Culture", Helsinki
National Pensions Institute, Helsinki

1953
Vogelweidplatz, sports centre and concert hall
(competition entry), Vienna, Austria

1954 ▸ The Aalto couple spends Christmas with
their friend Göran Schildt and sails on the River
Nile with the boat Daphne.
Studio Aalto, Munkkiniemi, Helsinki

1955 ▸ Aalto is appointed as a member of the
Finnish Academy.
Hansaviertel Block of Flats, Berlin, Germany
Church, Vuoksenniska, Imatra

1956 ▸ The Aalto couple travels to Venice for the
construction of the Finnish Pavilion.
Maison Louis Carré, Bazoches-sur-Guyonne,
France

1957 ▸ Aalto travels to England to accept the RIBA
gold medal awarded to him. He gives a lecture
about "Fighting architecture". An exhibition
dedicated to the cooperation of Alvar Aalto and
Mies van der Rohe takes place in Basel.

1958 ▸ Aalto's 60th birthday is celebrated so
heartily that a special permit to serve alcoholic
drinks must be obtained. He appears as a speaker
at the centenary celebrations of his school
Jyväskylän Lyseo (Jyväskylä Grammar School).
Town Hall (competition entry), Kiruna, Sweden
Town Centre, Seinäjoki
Neue Vahr Block of Flats, Bremen, Germany
Cultural Centre, Wolfsburg, Germany
Art Museum, Aalborg, Denmark

1959
Theatre, Essen, Germany
Enso-Gutzeit Headquarters, Helsinki
Church and Parish Centre, Wolfsburg, Germany
City Centre plan (not realised), Helsinki

1960 ▸ A large exhibition of Finnish architecture
takes places in Stockholm.
Municipal Library, Seinäjoki

1961 ▸ Aalto travels to the United States in order
to acquaint himself with warehouse architecture.
Municipal Library, Rovaniemi
Academic Bookshop, Helsinki
Town Centre, Rovaniemi

1962 ▸ Extensive exhibition in the museum
Central Finland about Aalto's work.
Finlandia Hall, Helsinki

1963 ▸ Appointment as chairman of the Finnish
Academy, a position Aalto keeps until 1968. He
compiles an extensive exhibition about his creations for the Berlin Academy of Arts. The exhibition travels further from Berlin to other European
countries and later to the USA. The American
Institute of Architects awards him a gold medal.
Aalto talks at the planning convention for Greater
Helsinki on "City planning and public buildings".

1964
Jyväskylä Administrative and Cultural Centre,
Jyväskylä

1965 ▸ Exhibition in the Palazzo Strozzi, which
comes to Helsinki and later in a scaled-down
version to Jyväskylä , then in 1969 to Sweden and
Brazil. The exhibition catalogue by Leonardo
Mosso presents Aalto's creations chronologically
for the first time.
Nordic House, Reykjavik, Iceland
Mount Angel Benedictine College Library,
Oregon, USA

1966
Cultural Centre (not realised), Siena, Italy
Church and Parish Centre, Riola di Vergato, Italy

1967 ▸ Aalto's last trip to the United States.
Villa Kokkonen, Järvenpää

1968 ▸ The Aalto couple is in Italy, and they cele-
brate Aalto's 70th birthday in Switzerland.

1969 ▸ The Aalto couple travels to Germany and
with Karl Fleig to Teheran.

Villa Schildt, Tammisaari
Art Museum (not realised), Shiraz, Iran

1971
Alvar Aalto Museum, Jyväskylä

1972 ▸ The Aalto couple travels to Paris to accept
the gold medal awarded by the Académie Française.
The exhibition "Alvar Aalto 50 ans de design" is
shown in Nice. In the next two years, the exhibition goes to Marseille, Paris, Mühlhausen, Metz,
Bordeaux and Brest.

1973 ▸ Exhibition of Aalto's creations in the
Museum of Finnish Architecture. In the new Alvar
Aalto Museum in Jyväskylä a retrospective Aalto
exhibition takes place. Inauguration of the
museum in September.

1975 ▸ Exhibition in Jyväskyla about forty years of
Artek, which afterward goes to the United States.

1976 ▸ Alvar Aalto dies on 11 May.

Europe

Bazoches-sur-Guyonne
Maison Carré
Berlin
Hansaviertel Block of Flats
Bremen
Neue Vahr Block of Flats
Espoo
Institute of Technology
Helsinki
Finlandia Hall
"House of Culture"

Residential Building and Studio
Imatra
Church of the Three Crosses
Jyväskylä
Workers' Club
Pedagogical University
Säynätsalo Town Hall
Kotka
Cellulose Factory and Housing Area
Muuratsalo
Experimental Summer House

Noormarkku
Villa Mairea
Paimio
Tuberculosis Sanatorium
Seinäjoki
Town Centre
Viipuri (Vyborg)
Municipal Library

Bibliography

▸ Alvar Aalto Houses. Timeless Expressions, A+U Architecture and Urbanism, June 1998. Extra edition
▸ Alvar and Aino Aalto as Glass Designers, Helsinki, 1996
▸ Blaser, Werner, Il Design di Alvar Aalto, Milan, 1981
▸ Fleig, Karl (Ed.), Alvar Aalto. Volume I 1922–62 (deutsch, français, english), Zurich, 1963
▸ Fleig, Karl (Ed.), Alvar Aalto. Volume II 1963–70 (deutsch, français, english), Zurich, 1971
▸ Fleig, Karl (Ed.), Alvar Aalto. Projekte und letzte Bauten. Volume III (deutsch, français, english), Zurich, 1978
▸ Gutheim, Frederick, Alvar Aalto. Masters of Modern Architecture, New York, 1960
▸ Heporauta, Arne (Ed.), Alvar Aalto. Arkkitehti/ Architect, Tampere, 1999
▸ Holma, M. and Lahti, M., Alvar Aalto. Elämälle herkempi rakenne. A gentler structure for Life. Eine sensiblere Struktur für das Leben. Una struttura più sensibile alla vita, Vammala, 1998
▸ Kapanen, M. and Mattila, S., Alvar Aalto ja Keski-Suomi. Alvar Aalto and Central Finland, Jyväskylä, 1985
▸ Koho, Timo, Alvar Aalto – Urban Finland, Tampere, 1997
▸ Korvenmaa, Pekka (Ed.), Sunila 1935–54. Alvar Aalto Architect: Vol. 7. Publ. by Alvar Aalto Foundation/Alvar Aalto Academy, Helsinki, 2004
▸ Laaksonen, Esa (Ed.), Drawn in Sand. Unrealised visions by Alvar Aalto, Helsinki, 2002
▸ Lahti, Louna, Alvar Aalto – Ex Intimo. Alvar Aalto through the Eyes of Family, Friends and Colleagues, Helsinki, 2001
▸ Muto, Akira, Alvar Aalto. La maison Louis Carré. Global Architecture, Tokyo, 1971
▸ Muto, Akira, Alvar Aalto. Church in Vuoksenniska. City Centre in Seinäjoki, Global Architecture, Tokyo, 1972
▸ Muto, Akira, Alvar Aalto. Town hall in Säynätsalo. Public Pensions Institute. Global Architecture, Tokyo, 1973
▸ Nerdinger, Winfried (Ed.), Alvar Aalto. Toward a Human Modernism, Landshut, 1999
▸ Paatero, Kristiina (Ed.), Viiva, Originaalipiirustuksia Alvar Aallon arkistosta. Linjen. Originalritningar ur Alvar Aaltos arkiv. The Line. Original Drawings from the Alvar Aalto Archive, Helsinki, 1993
▸ Pallasmaa, Juhani (Ed.), Alvar Aalto Furniture, Espoo, 1984
▸ Pallasmaa, Juhani (Ed.), The Aalto House 1935–36. Alvar Aalto Architect: Vol. 6. Publ. by Alvar Aalto Foundation/Alvar Aalto Academy, Helsinki, 2003
▸ Pearson, David, Alvar Aalto and the International Style, New York, 1989 (1978)
▸ Schildt, Göran, Alvar Aalto. A Life`s Work. Architecture, Design and Art, Keuruu, 1994
▸ Schildt, Göran, Alvar Aalto in his Own Words, Keuruu, 1997
▸ Schildt, Göran (Ed.), Alvar Aalto Sketches, Helsinki, 1978
▸ Spens, Michael, Alvar Aalto. Viipuri Library 1927–1935, London, 1994
▸ Tuukkanen, Pirkko (Ed.), Alvar Aalto Designer, Vammala, 2002
▸ Tzonis, Alexander (Ed.), The Architectural Drawings of Alvar Aalto 1917–1939, 1–12, New York, 1994
▸ Weston, Richard, Villa Mairea. Alvar Aalto, Hong Kong, 1992
▸ Weston, Richard, Town Hall in Säynätsalo. Alvar Aalto, Singapore, 1993
▸ Weston, Richard, Alvar Aalto, Hong Kong, 1995

Credits